Personal Knowledge Capital

CHANDOS
INFORMATION PROFESSIONAL SERIES

Series Editor: Ruth Rikowski
(email: Rikowskigr@aol.com)

Chandos' new series of books is aimed at the busy information professional. They have been specially commissioned to provide the reader with an authoritative view of current thinking. They are designed to provide easy-to-read and (most importantly) practical coverage of topics that are of interest to librarians and other information professionals. If you would like a full listing of current and forthcoming titles, please visit our web site www. chandospublishing.com or email wp@woodheadpublishing.com or telephone +44 (0) 1223 499140.

New authors: we are always pleased to receive ideas for new titles; if you would like to write a book for Chandos, please contact Glyn Jones on email gjones@chandospublishing.com or telephone number +44 (0) 1993 848726.

Bulk orders: some organisations buy a number of copies of our books. If you are interested in doing this, we would be pleased to discuss a discount. Please contact on email wp@woodheadpublishing.com or telephone +44 (0) 1223 499140.

Personal Knowledge Capital

The inner and outer path of knowledge creation in a web world

JANETTE YOUNG

CHANDOS
PUBLISHING

Oxford Cambridge New Delhi

Chandos Publishing
Hexagon House
Avenue 4
Station Lane
Witney
Oxford OX28 4BN
UK
Tel: +44 (0) 1993 848726
Email: info@chandospublishing.com
www.chandospublishing.com
www.chandospublishingonline.com

Chandos Publishing is an imprint of Woodhead Publishing Limited

Woodhead Publishing Limited
80 High Street
Sawston
Cambridge CB22 3HJ
UK
Tel: +44 (0) 1223 499140
Fax: +44 (0) 1223 832819
www.woodheadpublishing.com

First published in 2012

ISBN: 978-1-84334-700-2 (print)
ISBN: 978-1-78063-366-4 (online)

The right of Janette Young to be identified as the Author of this work has been asserted in accordance with sections 77 and 78 of the Copyright, Designs and Patents Act 1988

British Library Cataloguing-in-Publication Data.
A catalogue record for this book is available from the British Library.

Typeset by RefineCatch Limited, Bungay, Suffolk

This book is dedicated to
Sarah Elsie Young

Contents

List of figures and tables

Figures

Tables

Acknowledgements

I would like to thank those who have helped and supported me to complete this book. In particular, I would like to thank Professor David Wainwright for his support and constructive feedback. Thanks also go to Diane Young for her support at all times, and her editorial contribution. Thanks go to Dr Glyn Jones and the team at Chandos Publishing for their support. I would like to thank my family and friends for their unconditional love and support. I have written this book with my previous UK and international students in mind and I hope they enjoy and understand my message. I have on many occasions in the past been inspired by their feedback. This book is meant for them and the possibility that I could reach a wider audience. With love and thanks.

Dr Janette Young

Preface

This book has arisen because of my passion for my subject area of knowledge management and knowledge creation and the desire to further explore know-how and tacit knowledge in a web world. With over 15 years' experience as a senior lecturer in UK universities involved at postgraduate level, I had a wealth of experience to draw upon. I had previously designed and managed knowledge management postgraduate courses, including running one of the first MBA programmes in knowledge management in the UK at Anglia Ruskin University, followed later by an MSc in e-Knowledge Management. In this capacity, I taught both international and UK postgraduate students. After many years of managing and teaching modules in principles of knowledge management, knowledge and strategy, knowledge and technology, personal knowledge management and research methods, and working as an external examiner for three other UK universities, I felt it was time to express my own ideas in relation to the subject. My diverse and broad experience in this subject matter therefore informed my views. I currently work independently as a consultant. As an expert with a PhD in knowledge creation, my own ideas in relation to this theory are expressed in this book, supported by my qualitative empirical research investigation. Being research active and published in this area, I had presented at conferences in Europe and as far afield as Asia. In fact it was my first trip outside Europe to a conference in Asia that fully ignited my passion for personal awareness. Although always fascinated by the concept of tacit knowledge, my own personal journey into personal awareness began in 1996, and the result of this journey at this point in time is this book, blending together my interests, expertise in knowledge creation and personal awareness.

'Knowledge capital' brings a fresh and new perspective with its focus on valuing ideas and know-how. It is a journey that leads into the world of personal awareness as the search for 'know-how' unfolds into the realms of personal knowledge. At the same time we need to know how to communicate this knowledge and present it in order for it to reach the outside world. The idea for knowledge capital derives from knowledge management and knowledge creation theory, and can be viewed as part of personal knowledge management. The 'inner' and 'outer' paths of personal knowledge capital enable knowledge workers to create their own personal knowledge processes and take responsibility for their own development. Personal knowledge capital is an integration of inner knowledge and the exploitation of outer knowledge skills. This book attempts to take personal knowledge into new realms by focusing on the know-how and interior knowledge that forms part of the inner personal journey. In this way, individual personal knowledge is a search to understand and become aware of 'interior knowledge' as part of tacit knowledge and inner personal development.

The aim of the book is to integrate two paths, and blend the 'inner' with the 'outer' path in order to create personal knowledge capital. On the one hand, it aims to help individuals search for more understanding and meaning in the area of tacitness by linking to their own individual know-how; and on the other hand, the book hopes to emphasise the development of personal knowledge by successfully using web environments in order to do so. By discussing the link to networking, communities and various technologies the author hopes to embrace modern methods but at the same time be aware of the know-how within our own innate nature. By doing so, we can start to value our own inner knowledge, by using smart tools to express this knowledge. One way the reader can build personal knowledge capital and address his/her own limitations is by focusing on new and deeper elements of know-how and knowledge. In this way, the inner personal knowledge capital can, and does, reach greater levels of depth to support the interior world of the individual. This makes knowledge capital unique.

This book has been specifically written for the knowledge worker in the twenty-first-century organisation. It incorporates the development of a more fully developed set of ideas on knowledge creation theory to include the deeper levels of personal knowledge and how to communicate this knowledge within an increasingly virtual environment. The ideas in the book derive from my own research investigation into this subject area, whereby I highlighted that limitations existed on various levels within knowledge creation in relation to 'understanding personal know-how and tacit knowledge' and the creation of knowledge in a virtual environment. Eventually this analysis led me into the area of personal development. As such, I was inspired to rethink conceptually about the idea of personal knowledge for the knowledge worker. The tools and models put forward arise from a qualitative research investigation into knowledge creation using a knowledge-based web environment. This book focuses on sharing conversation, information and ideas, relationships, community and networking, and last but not least, harnessing the new interactive technologies.

The concept of personal knowledge capital falls into the category of third generation knowledge management with its focus on social capital. Personal knowledge capital forms part of knowledge creation theory for the virtual web environment within knowledge management theory, and it also overlaps into personal knowledge management. Because of this, personal knowledge capital is part of a new generation that integrates socio-technical, organic and personal development aspects. *Personal Knowledge Capital* attempts to engage an audience within business, knowledge management and management and the web environment who would not normally attempt to engage with, understand, or exploit this type of know-how. I hope that knowledge workers in the contemporary organisation can fully utilise all the skills and abilities available to them in the future, as well as utilising their own intuitive nature in order to address problems and issues that arise within their environment. Therefore, there is an emphasis on the knowledge worker using intuitive know-how to complement rational processes. The hope is that in the future these ideas and concepts will become the norm in organisations and that it will be considered acceptable practice for management to value intangible insights derived from the knowledge worker's inner reference system, so that this element may be valued and accepted as part of organisational practice. Personal knowledge capital would then be acknowledged and valued within forward-thinking creative organisations. Thus the interweaving of the 'inner and outer' path to knowledge could be integrated to include an approach to personal knowledge management and knowledge creation that fully exploits the individual's skills and abilities. The outcomes from my own research into web tools and technologies have resulted in the creation of an array of frameworks, models and design principles for exploiting knowledge creation, and social and intellectual capital through usage of web technologies. The emphasis here is on the use of the soft and interactive infrastructure provided by a web based system. Awareness of the value of intangible knowledge is a key theme throughout this book.

Chapters 1 and 2 introduce ideas associated with the development of individual personal knowledge and know-how and discuss how this can be fully developed. In particular, these ideas go into unfamiliar ground for management theory. Chapters 3 and 4 extend deeply into how knowledge workers can utilise their own personal inner guidance system for know-how, and Chapter 5 presents a new model and endeavours to extend the models and frameworks outlined by Nonaka and Takeuchi (1995) and Nonaka, Toyama and Konno (2000) by introducing new concepts and frameworks. Chapter 6 introduces the concept of network building, and by doing so, emphasises the development of intangible value. Chapter 7 examines social capital concepts to the reader, and explains issues of trust. Chapter 8 introduces the idea of the magic box metaphor and reminds us to value conversation in the knowledge creation process. Chapter 8, therefore, introduces the concept of ideas, conversation and culture for creating new knowledge and producing innovative solutions. Chapter 9 examines types of community that can be used when considering designing for a web environment. Chapter 10 proposes an infrastructure and tools and checklist that could be useful in the future to make best use of a knowledge-focused web environment for knowledge workers and online moderators. Chapter 11 examines knowledge creation in more depth and makes suggestion for the adaption of the model. Finally, Chapter 12 presents the Knowledge Cube as a visual metaphor to be used as a model for knowledge creation derived from a real world research investigation. The book concludes with a discussion on the inner and outer path for the knowledge worker in the contemporary organisation.

Janette Young, PhD

About the author

Dr Janette Young currently offers consultancy, coaching and training in knowledge management, innovative leadership, virtual learning and personal development to business professionals. She has worked for many years in higher education and was a Senior Lecturer with various UK Universities including Northumbria and Anglia Ruskin. In this capacity she managed, designed and taught on postgraduate programmes, including an MSc in e-Knowledge Management. At Anglia Ruskin University she developed close business relationships with local blue chip companies whilst acting as In-Company Corporate Director and designed one of the first UK MBA programmes in knowledge management. In this capacity she taught mainly post graduate UK and international students. In an international capacity she recruited for the University in Asia. On top of this she acted as an external examiner to three other UK Universities including Lincoln University; Robert Gordon University and Leeds Metropolitan University between 1997 and 2008. Janette's research expertise is in knowledge creation and web environment. As a researcher into knowledge creation Dr Young presented papers on the topic of knowledge management and knowledge creation at international conferences in Spain, Italy, Greece and India and has published in various international journals. She has acted as Associate Editor for Knowledge Management for various International Journals in Knowledge Management and was awarded two applauding learning and teaching awards from two Universities in 2003 and 2007. The author also has a keen interest in personal awareness development and continues to write in the subject area of knowledge creation. Janette lives in Northumberland in the North East of England in the UK. Contactable at informationknowledgefutures@gmail.com

Introduction to personal knowledge capital

Abstract: As we continually find ourselves living in and influenced by a technical web world, perhaps it is now time to look within ourselves for answers. This is at the heart of personal knowledge capital. The reader is introduced to the background of personal knowledge capital.

Key words: personal knowledge management, personal knowledge capital.

In the past few years in particular, we appear to be in a more complex and uncertain world, where major challenges have arisen. This world is increasingly dominated by technocrats, who have a set of rational needs, rather than being informed by their own ethical, moral and social inner world. We have stepped into the worst recession since the great depression; a roller-coaster of continuous natural disasters; and political unrest, including the Arab Spring. At a time of great turbulence in the world economically, socially, politically and environmentally, we all have a tendency to look to those in authority to find the answer and trust them to act on our behalf. At the heart of this are issues of integrity and honesty in all areas of life. How then can we all find answers to solve our problems? Those who hold high office may not live up to our own high ideals, standards and ethics. The answer is not to look outside, but rather to look within ourselves to find simple inner truth and thereby tap into our own integrity and honesty. We need to trust ourselves more on morals, ethics and beliefs, especially within the increasingly rational world we inhabit. By doing this, small steps can cause a ripple effect. The same applies to business solutions, as by going within, we may find the wisdom and answers. The knowledge worker, who is aware, may try to put this into effect. In an increasingly technological era, the idea of tapping into our own inner world of wisdom may seem at odds, but linking to our own emotional tacit knowledge can breed more creative ideas and solutions that ultimately lead to a more innovative environment in which to work. Today we are spending more time communicating and sharing experiences with others online, no matter where they reside. The latest tools enable social aspects of communicating that influence audiences at hereto unheard of super-speed. Sometimes in fact we rely too much on the outer voice. In a world of technological determinism, maybe it is time to step back, reflect, go inwards to feel and sense right solutions as opposed to increasingly looking outwards. Personal knowledge management tries to address the imbalance that has occurred - where many people almost worship every opinion announced through the new devices and technological gadgets available. It is time once again to tip the balance in favour of *what we feel*, rather than rely on outside influences.

This book has arisen because of my passion in the area of knowledge management: expertise in knowledge creation, research in the subject area and my desire to further explore know-how and tacit knowledge in a web world. The book explores the synthesis of mind and body in relation to tacit knowledge within knowledge creation theory. For the knowledge worker the book provides an alternative view of personal knowledge that endeavours to offer insight into developing 'know-how'. As such, a new model for the inner path is presented as part of knowledge creation theory. For the academic and business professional, it builds on knowledge creation theory to inform through new models and tools. For the knowledge professional, the book explores third generation knowledge management with a focus on social and intellectual capital in relation to the web environment. For the web designer and academic alike, the book presents principles, tools, frameworks and models grounded in real-world research. For the knowledge worker, academic and student, reflective steps are offered to develop personal awareness. The book offers the knowledge worker a set of tools for personal knowledge awareness.

The greatest power is non-visible and intangible. In the twenty-first-century organisation, knowledge is power. However, it is not the knowledge that counts, it is what you do with it that is key. The concept of personal knowledge capital blends the inner element of personal know-how to the outer environment, thereby linking deep inner knowing and external forms of communicating that knowledge through the use of technology. By blending inner and outer knowledge, knowledge workers are able to go deep within themselves to tap into their inner knowingness and listen for solutions, and thereafter explicitly communicate this within an increasingly virtual environment. The next sections outline the background to this subject area.

Knowledge management and knowledge creation

Knowledge management has become a valuable management theory introduced in the late twentieth century with a focus on tacitness and placing value on the intangibles. As will be exemplified throughout the book, Nonaka and Takeuchi are leading writers on knowledge creation and are highly respected within the field. Their book *The knowledge creating company* (1995) presented a view that encompasses an Eastern Japanese flavour that focuses on the soft rather than hard side of management. Their models and frameworks are discussed across the world, and their work has been up-dated by Nonaka and Konno (1998) and Nonaka, Toyama and Konno (2000) as will be illustrated later in the book. Nonaka and Takeuchi (1995) fully discuss 'a number of false dichotomies' in their approach to management including a split between:

- tacit/explicit
- mind/body
- individual/organisations
- top-down/bottom-up
- bureaucracy/task force
- relay/rugby
- East/West.

It is the aim of this book to explore the integration of mind versus body in relation to tacit knowledge within the domain of knowledge creation theory and by doing so focus on the 'inner path'. In the West the tradition was to separate body and mind, and this was referred to as a Cartesian split or dualism (Nonaka and Takeuchi 1995). The synthesis of the two opposing sides of the dualism was dubbed 'the oneness of body and mind' by Eisai, one of the founders of Zen Buddhism in medieval Japan (Nonaka and Takeuchi 2005). Nonaka and Takeuchi placed a strong emphasis on bodily experience from three modes of knowledge creation arising from pure or direct experience such as subjective insights, intuitions and bodily experience; areas not deeply explored. We are today much more attuned to oneness of body and mind thinking in the West, but how it operates, and where and at what level in knowledge creation, requires further exploration. In the West we still tend to over-emphasise the importance of explicit knowledge over tacit knowledge; however, in the past decade the gap has narrowed as knowledge management thinking has done much to reverse this trend. In terms of management style there is still too much emphasis placed on individualism over collaborative behaviour. However, it is the first step in the exploration of the oneness of body and mind thinking within knowledge creation that begins in Part 1 (*The inner path of knowledge creation*).

The knowledge worker

It was Drucker (1999) who coined the term 'knowledge worker'. This influential management writer spearheaded a decade of discussion on the role of the knowledge worker within the knowledge economy. Today, knowledge workers need an array of skills at their fingertips to enable them to use the tangible and intangible elements all around them. The knowledge worker is essentially a key player at the heart of effective organisational performance, and as such should make best possible use of all the routes and technological tools at his or her disposal. In a world where work involves interacting in the physical and virtual space, keeping pace with the latest developments can be stressful and knowledge workers may find themselves out of kilter in terms of the work–life balance or mind and body integration as they strive to keep all the elements together. In other words, the knowledge worker has a lot to contend with in an increasingly fast technological world where speed is valued and traditional values are questioned. Because of this, this book suggests a number of steps the knowledge worker can take to step back and reflect on who they are and what they want to achieve in the work environment, and by doing so reclaim their own self-mastery.

Knowledge management in a web environment

Knowledge management theory has developed to span a wide range of disciplines, drawing upon many theories and methodologies, resulting in a spectrum of competing definitions and perspectives. The wide-ranging interdisciplinary nature of knowledge management with its emphasis on intangible aspects within management makes the theory imperative for the twenty-first-century management professional. Knowledge management theory was initially viewed from a knowledge and technology perspective in the 1990s when the theory first emerged and was linked to the storage of information and knowledge in systems. Thus in the early days a hard systems approach was taken, with little discussion related to the softer aspects of tacit knowledge. In the late 1990s as internet access and technological tools were rapidly developing, the theory developed from the storage of knowledge within computer-based systems to human and behavioural aspects which finally led to a focus on intellectual capital. As knowledge management theory developed it moved on to focus on culture, people and social interactions, with greater value being placed on these areas. Because of this, knowledge management can be viewed as first, second and third generation (McElroy 2003). The first generation is the link to storage and systems; the second generation focuses on valuing human aspects; and the third generation emphasises valuing the intangibles and intellectual capital. Third generation knowledge management is at the heart of this book due to its emphasis upon linking social capital to the web technologies.

As technology continues to develop at breakneck speed – inclusive of new features and interoperability capabilities – we all often find ourselves needing to catch up with the latest features. The web environment allows for fast forms of communication in the workplace while the speed at which we constantly communicate means we currently utilise the web, mobile technology and communications on a daily basis. Knowledge workers at the forefront may find that they need to continually acquire new skills to keep pace with the latest developments. It is, therefore, important for the individual knowledge worker to skilfully employ these new tools and skills for increased efficiency, creativity and innovation. The web environment itself means that the knowledge worker is continually working within both physical and virtual space and as such operates in a dynamic environment using an increasingly connected array of information and communication tools. Because of this, the knowledge worker is able to be more flexible and autonomous.

We need to be able to see the web environments not only from the point of view of information and communication tools, but also from the point of view of tools for knowledge creation: knowledge sharing, knowledge distribution and social interaction. By doing so, we are developing a more rounded approach to the potential of the technologies, and showing an aptitude for continuous creative innovative solutions to problems and issues. Thus through altering the lens the view widens. In particular, it may be difficult to use theory to conceptually understand the new features in operation, as there is very often a lag between practice and theory. Later chapters in this book reveal some of the emerging conceptual and theoretical principles as we examine the web environment from the point of view of knowledge creation. As we do this, we see that the principles of knowledge management (including knowledge distribution and knowledge creation) can be identified, balanced and integrated into everyday activities. The issues are fully discussed to cover the concept of external knowledge capital and, in particular, highlight how the softer interactive aspects within the web environment can be mobilised to form the *pièce de résistance*, in order to secure intangible value. An awareness of the powerful value and benefits arising from knowledge systems, and an appreciation of the most suitable tools and models to support this practice, can help the knowledge worker produce creative solutions in the workplace. In essence, the tools for personal knowledge management need to combine the need for managing personal knowledge (the PKM paradigm) with the requirement for developing virtual knowledge creation through the web environment (with a socio-technical approach to systems). One way to do this is to focus on the exploitation of social and intellectual capital through using virtual communities and web tools and technologies in a web environment.

In exploring knowledge management and the technologies, it appears that much focus has been upon the storage of knowledge within the technologies rather than on the creation of new knowledge. Because of this, the design processes to support the infrastructures for the softer aspects of knowledge creation and the technologies are rare, and therefore, the emphasis in this book is upon redressing this balance, particularly in the later chapters. The outer aspects of knowledge capital are explored and show the knowledge worker how to make best use of his/her networks and technologies to professionally exploit their own knowledge. Personal knowledge capital (PKC) is the 'know-how' that results from inner awareness, intuitive processes, selective thinking patterns, reflective practice and the exploitation of the web and personal knowledge practices, to support the endeavours of the knowledge worker. Knowledge capital delves into the area of personal knowledge management theory, and binds all of the above together by usage of the web technologies.

Personal knowledge management

Within the multidisciplinary field of knowledge management, an area known as personal knowledge management (PKM) has developed with an emphasis on individuals taking personal responsibility for their development. Many of the writers in the PKM area do not necessarily agree on a consensus for personal knowledge management due to its interdisciplinary nature. Interdisciplinary PKM is defined as the 'bringing together and interweaving of content, methods, and research strategies of various existing fields of study' (Payne 1999, p. 176, cited in Jones 2009). This allows a mode of enquiry that draws from the knowledge bases of many disciplines, enabling scholars to see from different viewpoints. Under the umbrella of personal knowledge management, Jones (2009) suggests that PKM invites an approach to knowledge management (KM) that encourages organisations to facilitate workers to take responsibility for managing information and increasing their own productivity, through a variety of tools and techniques (Jefferson 2006, cited in Jones 2009). PKM as a subject area has been explored by writers such as Cope (2000), who discusses personal knowledge in terms of head, heart and hand. Where head can be linked to the cognitive processes, heart can be linked to the intuition and hand represents the actions and behaviour taken. Cope's work takes a distinctive approach to the subject by making a serious attempt to discuss inner knowledge, unlike the other writers on the subject who are more focused on the information and communication aspects of knowledge with the emphasis on knowledge storage.

Although early efforts in PKM have focused on how individuals use technology to manage information, recent studies (Miller 2005, cited in Jones 2009) emphasise the role of dynamic work environments in motivating employees to manage their personal knowledge in a way that combines it with organisational needs. How the individual builds his or her own knowledge base is an important question, deserving further examination (Truch 2001). Wright (2005) proposed that PKM involves a combination of cognitive, informational, social, learning and development competencies, which individuals draw on to function effectively in the workplace. From this perspective Wright believes the goal of understanding PKM is to enable individuals to operate successfully in highly volatile, information-rich and technologically advanced organisations. Doong and Wang (2008) take a learning perspective to PKM, believing that the goal is to help individuals to create, organise and make available important knowledge. Thus for them, personal knowledge management systems (PKMS) are important to an individual's daily life, because whenever a person wants to learn something new or search for potentially useful information, a PKMS will help them to achieve these objectives in a more effective and efficient way through technology. In this way, PKM invites an approach that encourages organisations to facilitate workers to take responsibility by using knowledge systems effectively.

The key issues support knowledge workers 'managing and supporting personal knowledge and information so that it is accessible, meaningful and valuable to the individual; maintaining networks, contacts and communities; making life easier and more enjoyable; and exploiting personal capital' (Higgison 2004, cited in Agnihotri and Troutt 2009). Despite all of the above approaches to personal knowledge management, only Cope really attempts to understand the emotional aspects of personal knowledge. Because of this, in particular, there is space for further examination of personal knowledge management to incorporate the inner individual emotional and cognitive elements of knowledge creation theory.

Introduction to personal knowledge capital

Personal knowledge capital is an idea deriving from knowledge creation theory and is part of personal knowledge management. Exploring the area of individual tacit knowledge, knowing and know-how in knowledge creation theory, highlighted the need to try to understand in depth inner tacit knowledge. The theory of knowledge creation seemed to dry up at this point, and most writers turned to the work of Polanyi (1966) to define the area in greater depth. The ideas in the book arose as a way to partly address the limitations in this area, by advocating personal development awareness as a developing element within the theory. The intention is to introduce the knowledge professional to the deep inner aspects of knowledge creation by exploring the area of 'know-how'. Personal knowledge capital as a concept highlights the value of tacitness in the shape of know-how, insight, ideas and emotion so they can be shared between individual knowledge workers in organisations. Thus the emphasis is upon the knowledge worker continuing to develop their own unique personal value added, thereby adding individual creativity and innovation to their working practice. This book *Personal Knowledge Capital* shows how this can be revealed, developed and exploited to create new insight for the professional knowledge worker. As such, knowledge capital examines the whole area of personal 'know-how' as part of the intangible aspects of knowledge creation theory, and therefore places a greater emphasis on the inner intuitive aspects for the individual knowledge worker.

Outer knowledge capital highlights areas where intangible value can be fully exploited from trust within relationship building to online design and community interactions. It discusses areas we need to understand in order to create tangible value-added from 'intangible form'.

Summary

The author has discussed the background to her research into knowledge creation. We have discussed the arrival of the knowledge worker in the late twentieth and early twenty-first centuries, the interdisciplinary nature of knowledge management, and the arrival of PKM inclusive of the web environment. In this new era, the waves of new web tools and technologies are fast and furious and lead to new ways of operating within the firm. Personal knowledge capital is of particular interest to the knowledge worker in an increasingly dominant technological environment, as it explores an inner and outer path. In Part 1 we will examine the ability of the knowledge worker to use their inner personal knowledge, and in Part 2 on the outer path we will examine how this can be exploited by examining our current environment through networks, conversation, social capital and design for knowledge creation in web environments. Chapter 2 begins with an exploration of the nature of tacitness and know-how within knowledge creation.

Part 1
The inner path of knowledge creation

The greatest power is non-visible and intangible

In the contemporary organisation, knowledge is power! 'The inner path' is a series of chapters that take you on a journey that enables you to understand tacit knowledge. This inner journey suggests you should go deep inside for creative solutions and suggests methods and tools that you may use in order to do so. The final chapter results in the creation of a new model for the inner journey, and thereby extends the SECI model of knowledge creation.

2

Exploring knowledge creation and tacit knowledge

Abstract: Tacit knowledge as part of knowledge management and knowledge creation is the most interesting and fascinating of areas to examine. Tacit knowledge is what makes knowledge management theory so unique. Because of this, the SECI model is crucial to knowledge creation theory as it explores the interactions between tacit and explicit knowledge. In fact, there is no split between tacit and explicit knowledge, but rather a continuum between these two discrete dimensions. This chapter examines the SECI model of knowledge creation, knowingness and know-how in greater detail.

Key words: SECI model, knowingness, know-how.

While the twentieth-century management paradigm was all about control, efficiency and the bottom line in terms of costs, the twenty-first-century modern management paradigm widens its focus to incorporate a variety of elements that suggest that intangible value in the form of valuing smart and collaborative working practices has a much higher priority. At the core of knowledge management is Nonaka and Takeuchi's work (Nonaka 1991; Nonaka and Takeuchi 1995) on knowledge creation where the focus was to blend a Japanese perspective with a Western tradition. They discuss the integration of the teachings of Buddhism and Confucianism with management culture and major Western philosophical thought. In particular, the Japanese perspective focuses on the themes of 'oneness of humanity and nature' with an emphasis on living in the present, and on oneness of 'body and mind'. You can see this type of language and labels arising throughout their work. In many ways their work at the time was a break with traditional Western management approaches and brought with it a fresh and new perspective. Throughout this book we will aim to continue to discuss the 'body and mind' theme and expand upon this trait.

Knowledge creation and SECI

Knowledge creation theory is at the heart of knowledge management. It has enabled the processes of knowledge to be broken down into understandable parts. The theory of knowledge creation has been led by the work of Nonaka (1991) and Nonaka and Takeuchi (1995). Nonaka and Takeuchi's theory has achieved paradigmatic status since the mid-1990s (Gourlay 2006), and it has been described as one of the best and most influential models in knowledge strategy literature (Choo and Bontis 2002, cited in Gourlay 2006), and as highly respected (Easterby-Smith and Lyles 2003, cited in Gourlay 2006). As this theory has become so highly regarded, we need to understand the theory in further detail, so as to make best use of it as we continue to advance into the twenty-first century. In order to understand knowledge creation it is crucial to have an understanding not only of the explicit dimension, but of the tacit dimension of knowledge creation. Explicit knowledge is that which can be articulated and written down: it is stored and repackaged knowledge. Explicit knowledge is more than information and data in that it brings greater insights to storage of information. However, it is an awareness of the value of the tacit dimension which makes knowledge management theory so unique An awareness of this concept – sometimes 'sticky' and rather difficult to define – is crucial for managers so that they can use and value the intangibles within the organisation. Having a discussion about the intangible is equally important when we consider this concept in terms of developing web technologies in the virtual dimension. We need to understand how the knowledge worker facilitates this intangible element within organisations and through personal usage of the technologies. Within the theory it is in fact the tacit dimension that is the most elusive element to pin down.

At the centre of Nonaka and Takeuchi's (1995) and Nonaka, Toyama and Konno's (2000) theory of knowledge creation is the SECI model where knowledge develops from the interactions between tacit and explicit knowledge in all four sections of the model. Within the model (see Fig 2.1 for full explanation) *S* stands for socialisation – the sharing of experiences between individuals; *E* indicates externalisation – articulating tacit knowledge into explicit concepts; *C* denotes combination – systemising concepts into a knowledge system combining different bodies of explicit knowledge, and *I* stands for internalisation – embodying explicit knowledge into tacit knowledge through learning by doing. Each area of the model links to a type of characteristic: socialisation links to empathy; externalisation to articulating; combination to connecting and internalisation to embodying. There is an evolving spiral movement occurring in and between the four processes of SECI. This starts at the individual level and expands out across the organisation. This spiral represents the expansion of knowledge creation. The model is in effect an attempt to break down the processes by which knowledge creation occurs. To begin any discussion on knowledge creation it is necessary first to explore the meaning of knowledge and the concept of tacitness which defines the knowledge creation theory within knowledge management.

	Tacit Knowledge	To	Explicit Knowledge
Tacit Knowledge	(Socialisation) **Sympathised Knowledge**		(Externalisation) **Conceptual Knowledge**
From			
Explicit Knowledge	(Internalisation) **Operational Knowledge**		(Combination) **Systemic Knowledge**

Figure 2.1 **The SECI model**
Source: After Nonaka, I and Takeuchi, H (1995). Reproduced with permission from Oxford University Press, from Fig. 3.4 'Contents of Knowledge created by the Four Modes' in Nonaka, I and Takeuchi, H (1995), *The Knowledge Creating Company: How Japanese Companies Create the Dynamics of Innovation*, p 72

Tacit knowledge conversion at the core of Nonaka's theory of organisational knowledge creation is clearly focused on the conversion of the tacit knowledge of performing individuals, teams and groups within organisations and institutions (Garcia 2009). If tacit knowledge conversion is at the heart of the knowledge management discipline, then understanding the deeper realms of individual tacitness is important to understanding how the principles and processes stretch out to reach the group and organisational levels.

Tacitness and the cognitive and technical elements

The early founders of knowledge creation, Nonaka and Takeuchi (1995), introduced tacit knowledge to management, inviting an appreciation of tacitness, involving both a cognitive and a technical dimension. They suggest that once the importance of tacit knowledge is realised, then we begin to think about innovation in a whole new way as part of a highly individual process of personal and organisational self-renewal. Tacitness starts at the individual level within the knowledge worker. As such, the emphasis is upon new knowledge being a process of ongoing personal and organisational self-renewal where knowledge has to be built on its own, frequently requiring intensive and laborious interactions among members of the organisation (Nonaka and Takeuchi 1995). This early discussion of tacit knowledge has an almost Zen feel about it as they highlight the importance of transcending a multitude of dichotomies including body versus mind. They highlight the point that tacit knowledge needs to be recognised not as a machine for processing information but as a living organism. Their emphasis upon tacit knowledge is placed upon highly subjective insights, intuitions, and hunches and they suggest that it also embraces ideas, values and emotions, images and symbols. According to Nonaka, Toyama and Konno (2000), tacit knowledge is deeply rooted in action, procedures, routines, commitment, ideals, values and emotions. This view of tacit knowledge is important as it embraces emotions, as well as images. In terms of emotions, tacit knowledge may be based on a subjective insight or hunch. An emphasis on the emotional aspect of tacit knowledge will be covered in the next two chapters. Each aspect of the SECI model may link to knowledge assets as discussed in a later chapter. In particular, socialisation within the SECI model loosely links to experiential knowledge assets in the unified theory of knowledge creation. One area of knowledge assets rarely fully acknowledged is emotional knowledge assets. Indeed, this is an area to explore further along with emotional tacit knowledge. As will be argued in this book, emotional knowledge in particular forms a strong element within personal knowledge capital.

Nonaka and Takeuchi (1995) stress that the *cognitive* element of tacit knowledge pertains to an individual's images of reality and visions for the future, suggesting that the articulation of tacit perspectives is a kind of 'mobilization' process for the creation of new knowledge. This cognitive dimension may centre on mental models, which include schemata, paradigms, beliefs, viewpoints and perspectives. According to Nonaka et al. the cognitive dimension of tacit knowledge reflects our image of reality – the what is, and what ought to be, elements. However, they suggest that these elements cannot be articulated very easily, because these implicit models shape the way we perceive the world around us. The cognitive dimension exists and is discussed only vaguely, and this suggests an area that could be more fully examined. This aspect will be further explored in more detail in Chapter 4. On the other hand, the *technical* dimension as discussed by Nonaka et al. is informal, hard to pin down skills or craft captured in the term 'know-how'. Nonaka, Byosiere, Borucki and Konno (1994) emphasise that the technical element of tacit knowledge covers concrete know-how, crafts and skills that apply to specific contexts. The technical dimension may encompass learning technical knowledge from non-verbal observation. An example given revolves around the master craftsman who has a high level of expertise but struggles to articulate this. Therefore, an apprentice chef may have to learn his craft by observational procedures. Non-verbal communication in this sense is very important to the socialisation process. Here we have concrete 'know-how' being discussed, but little mention is made of an intuitive inner 'know-how' that individuals may perceive. Once again, this is an area which could be further examined. Although Nonaka and Takeuchi (1995) talk about a cognitive and technical dimension to tacit knowledge, it is the notion of tacitness and its relation to 'knowing' that is one of the most interesting aspects of knowledge creation. Know-how, although briefly discussed in knowledge creation theory, seems to be an area which may not necessarily be limited to a technical or cognitive dimension, and indeed it could be more fully explored to include a personal awareness dimension. This is especially the case when we relate to emotional tacit knowledge. Knowledge creation, know-how and knowingness are further explored in the next section.

Knowledge creation, knowingness and know-how

Examining knowledge creation theory in depth leads into the area of 'knowingness' and 'know-how' as part of the SECI model within knowledge creation (Figure 2.1). Knowledge management academic writers have talked about the idea of 'knowing' but rarely seem to have discussed the concept in detail. If you explore this fascinating area, it may lead you into new avenues and directions in terms of self-awareness and consciousness (a 'mind–body' perspective). In doing so, we will look at the theoretical aspects, before moving on to discuss this in terms of our own awareness. As knowledge management and knowledge creation theory mention the concept of 'know-how' the question arising is: how does the knowledge worker define and access this concept at the individual personal level? Indeed, this is a difficult area to get 'a handle on'. Nonaka (1991), Nonaka and Takeuchi (1995) and Nonaka, Toyama and Konno (2000) discuss 'know-how' as part of knowledge creation in their SECI model (Figure 2.1). The SECI model emphasises tacit-to-tacit 'socialisation' processes within the model where individuals glean knowledge from observation, or through discussion. In this way they acquire knowledge through discussion with colleagues both formally and informally, or through tacit-to-tacit discussion between individuals one-to-one or one-to-many. As part of this process, personal tacit knowledge can arise from one-to-one conversation, where ideas are discussed and insights, hints and tips are shared and evaluated, and, if appropriate, where new ideas emerge to create new mental models and ways of thinking. This is part of tacit knowledge acquired in daily life. Conversation is thus a major element in tacitness. Added to this, knowledge can be acquired implicitly through a type of non-verbal communication such as making use of metaphors as a way of describing a situation. Thus you may find people metaphorically describing a event. This is a very subtle way of communicating. However, Nonaka and Takeuchi do not make a distinction between tacitness and implicitness and – as Li and Gao (2003) highlight – what they mean by tacitness actually includes implicitness. This is because implicit knowledge can include the use of metaphors and imagery as a way of communicating. However, there is a level of knowledge in terms of knowledge creation defined, and this is 'know-how and knowingness' starting at the individual level. This suggests an opportunity to further analyse this concept. Although Nonaka and Takeuchi talk about a cognitive and a technical dimension, it is the 'notion' of knowing in terms of tacitness that is one of the most interesting aspects.

Within knowledge creation, 'knowing' is a complex concept that needs to be explored at a deeper level. In earlier work, Polanyi (1966; 1983) introduced the concept of 'knowing', which was not directly related to the introduction of the recent theory of knowledge management. However, their theory is relevant as it recognises the innate tacit knowledge that as individuals we 'don't know what we know'. This type of 'don't know what we know' thinking is part of the core element of tacit knowledge. The implication is that this is a type of individual sensing of deep knowing which arises from instinct rather than relating to thoughts. Polanyi's perspective acknowledges both a 'tacit' and an 'explicit' dimension, and he highlights what he calls a 'continuum' between tacit and explicit knowledge, rather than viewing each concept as a separate entity. Polanyi also suggests that we should reconsider human knowledge by starting from the point that we may know more than we can tell. He questions whether we may have a tacit 'foreknowledge' of yet undiscovered things. Polanyi's tacit dimension refers to innate intelligence, perception and capability for reasoning, rather than a type of memory storage. In this way, according to Polanyi, we can be aware of hidden implications. He suggests that this type of knowledge may be 'instinctive' knowledge that may arise in the rich knowledge that is available – but sometimes only if we are prepared to listen. This type of 'know-how' is individual and involves reaching down and recognising a level of awareness and consciousness that works at a deep level within the individual. Polanyi emphasises that in terms of the pursuit of knowledge, we are at all times 'guided by sensing the presence of a hidden reality' towards which clues are pointing. The way we exercise our tacit powers of 'knowing' suggests that the things that we know include problems and hunches, physiognomies and skills, the use of tools, probes, and denotative language, and any list extended all the way to include the primitive knowledge of external objects perceived by our senses (Polanyi 1966; 1983). According to Polanyi, 'knowing' relies on 'interiorizing particulars' to which we are not attending and which, therefore, we may not be able to specify. He suggests that this relies on our attending to unspecifiable particulars and connecting to them in a way we cannot define. This type of thinking lends itself to Sartre's work on consciousness and being (Sartre 1976, cited in Boyle 2005) which highlights layers of consciousness available at a deep level in individuals who are 'awake enough' to tap into their own 'knowing' elements. Sartre's thinking suggests that the mind and thinking are external reasoning mechanisms but not necessarily the real 'knowing self' which can be listened to and discovered in the interior silence of individuals. We can deduce from this that relying on knowing at the individual level falls within the realms of a type of tacitness of individual personal knowledge. The suggestion is that acting on this 'knowing' can give access to deep realms of knowledge from within the individual.

There is a link between Polanyi's original ideas on 'individual and personal knowing and interiorising' and concept of tacitness formulated by Nonaka and co-authors (1991; 1995; 2000) as part of the know-how within tacit knowledge. These two views on knowledge have some overlap, but while Polanyi focuses on the instinctive and sensory elements of individual knowing, Nonaka and his colleagues focus on tacit knowledge as part of a set of processes within the SECI framework which they use to examine knowledge creation in organisations. Although 'knowing' is implied within any discussion of tacitness in the knowledge creation theory, Nonaka and Takeuchi (1995) do not delve deeply into this aspect, or emphasise the uniqueness of the role that individual 'knowingness' plays in relation to knowledge creation. It is useful for knowledge creation processes to be broken down into understandable elements in order to understand these processes in more detail; however, as we do so, this unleashes the limitations of the model presented by Nonaka et al. Nevertheless, identifying tacit know-how in more depth may further enable the development of this area. Of course, further examination of know-how eventually leads down the personal development route within personal knowledge, and shows deeper individual elements not discussed within Nonaka's definition of tacit knowledge, thereby unveiling a deeper and more practical level of 'knowingness' and 'know-how'. Having an awareness of the limitations of the theory, and expanding it to acknowledge and value 'know-how' at the individual level as a sensing inner truth, may ultimately help the organisation achieve greater value. Thus this process may allow knowledge workers and leaders to embrace a less mechanical, or a more intuitive, style of decision-making process in the corporate workplace in order to enhance creativity and innovation.

Summary

We have discussed the arrival of knowledge management theory on the corporate agenda from the mid-1990s onwards. Because of this, tacitness has been valued highly in the process of innovation. In particular, personal knowledge is still an area that is developing and the dimensions of individual cognitive and technical tacitness may include 'emotional know-how'. As we value the intangibles in all forms within the field of knowledge management, it appears that tacitness at a deep level of intuitive knowledge and knowing has not been fully explored, and, this book attempts to address the issue by examining this element more fully. In doing so, this concept links to personal development and is another example of the multi-disciplinary approach to the subject of knowledge management. The question is: How does the individual knowledge worker identify and develop his/her intangible knowledge for creative, innovative and smart working practices? What are effective ways to communicate knowingness within the organisation at both the individual and group level? In the next chapter we will look at knowingness in greater detail.

3

Tuning-in: knowingness for inner personal knowledge capital

Abstract: The need for 'oneness of body and mind' underpins the Eastern intellectual tradition and from this perspective, knowledge means wisdom that is acquired from the perspective of the whole personality. This chapter continues to explore inner emotional tacit knowledge.

Key words: tuning-in, personal knowledge capital, knowingness, interiorisation, knowing, intuitive solutions.

'You do not have to acquire anything; you only have to *know*'. *Paramahansa Yogananda*

Do you want an answer to a really important question? Do you want to go in the right direction, and find the right solution? Does anyone ever tell you to go within yourself for the answer? It seems that all these answers are 'out there', and the world has only an external reality. In fact, your own world is made up of a mix of internal and external reality. Understanding that you need to go inside yourself for answers is a huge step forward in terms of your future success. In this respect, personal knowledge capital differs from other theories as it encompasses the exploration of an inner and outer level within knowledge creation. The inner path supports self awareness through knowledge creation. Capital is a word that means gaining value. As we look at the personal capital of the individual knowledge worker we are going to focus on the individual 'inner guidance system' in order to gain more insight. Knowing what knowledge we have is not always easy. Tacit knowledge even at the individual level is mainly an untapped and under-utilised resource. However, for the knowledge worker at the individual level, this becomes increasingly important as we enter an era where intangible value continues to be highly valued. With this in mind, this whole area of tacitness and, in particular, know-how needs to be further explored in greater detail.

Nonaka and Takeuchi (1995) highlight three distinctions of the Japanese intellectual tradition including 'oneness of humanity and nature'; 'oneness of body and mind'; and 'oneness of self and other'. They stress that these traits form the foundation of the Japanese view towards knowledge as well as the Japanese approach towards management practice. This view is in contrast to the more rational approach taken in the West towards management. Nonaka and Takeuchi stress that knowledge means wisdom that is acquired from the perspective of the entire personality, and they emphasise that this orientation has provided a basis for valuing personal and physical experience over indirect, intellectual abstraction. The need for 'oneness of body and mind' underpins the Eastern intellectual tradition. Indeed, Nonaka and Takeuchi mention that this is the ultimate tradition for Zen practitioners to seek, by means of internal meditation and disciplined life. Therefore, by examining deeply inner personal knowledge to include 'oneness of body and mind' as developed through personal awareness, the knowledge worker can complement rational ways of viewing things in the workplace with inner intuitive knowing. This chapter discusses how you might go about doing this and, in the process, delve inside yourself to discover emotional tacit knowledge creation.

Living and sensing

Although 'knowingness' in terms of an inner 'sensing' of what we as individuals already know, and bringing it to the forefront, has been acknowledged in an earlier chapter, we still need to understand how to access this deep inner knowledge. As discussed, Nonaka and Takeuchi (1995) mention emotional tacit knowledge but there are few examples in their theory of knowledge creation. Indeed, inner sensing is part of listening to the body's knowingness. Can you hear yourself say at times, 'I just know'? as physiological 'feelings' may alert us to knowingness. It is the knowing deep in the gut that acts as a type of calling card. You can feel it, when sometimes you get 'stirrings in the gut' telling you what is imminent. You need to listen to these feelings as they come from the real you. It is your greater self being unleashed. Those who go against their own 'inner prompt' level may betray their true nature and this ultimately makes life more difficult in the future. This is because you have gone against your true self. Those who grasp this meaning, and live by their true inner nature, when it reveals itself, are going with the flow of their own truth and thereby living their own song. As you do so you develop your intuitive side, and more and more of this part of your very being will be revealed to you. Animals are a good example of creatures who live by sensing and instinct. For example, in the tsunami in Sri Lanka, the animals were seen running for the hills long before the tsunami hit the island. The instinct of animals is far more naturally honed-in than that of humans. While animals have instinct, we humans tend to have not only instinct but a more refined access to what we call intuition. Indeed, it is widely reported that Nobel Prize winners use intuition as an important part of creative and scientific discoveries. We humans have allowed the external world to curb our natural intuitive tendencies, and because of this we can be crushed by focusing on the external reality that others tend to tell us is the real world. An awareness of our own natural inner nature may in fact save our lives (intuition, as discussed here, relates to the body's natural 'knowing feelings'). Why then is no one shouting this from the roof-tops and telling us to develop our true natural nature that guides us for the greater good? When we do this we link to our own body awareness, as part of the 'oneness of body and mind' as mentioned in the knowledge creation theory.

The inner realm

The concept and process of inner personal capital arises to help the knowledge worker look inside for answers and solutions, rather than without. How do you find answers to those unknown questions? How do you make good decisions that are profound? The answer is that you go 'within'. Why are we always taught to listen to what other people have to say, rather than becoming our own sub-guru? Why externalise rather than internalise? Don't look for all the answers outside any more, rather learn to listen to that quiet inner voice – the one we often try to suppress because we are too busy listening to our mind or our logic. Why does no one ever teach us to listen to our own inner self – our divine spark? Why didn't anyone teach us that we too have antenna, an inner voice which we can tap into? This level of communication to the hidden intelligence with the 'you that you are', may partly be communication at a deeper level which forms into an 'inner spark'. This enables us to tap into and access the 'know what we don't know' at a subconscious level. This 'gut feel' links to the whole person's feelings and deep levels of awareness, although we may not be sure where it comes from as it is intangible and it forms part of our individual know-how and knowingness. This is your 'inner guidance' system that forms part of your deeper inner consciousness. Therefore, inner 'know-how' is found deep within the individual, available like a compass to self-direct. It links to hunches, and attentive listening, and forms part of the divine spark and presence. This quiet observation allows us to align to our own inner knowledge and helps us to develop 'self awareness'. How come it is rarely ever mentioned in any shape or form in our schooling, religion, philosophy or management science? What we are not taught is to 'listen' or spend quiet time in the stillness. Listen to the still quiet voice within. In personal knowledge creation terms listening to bodily awareness is important.

Acknowledging and listening to your own internal 'knowing', may provide greater levels of guidance for you in order to support innovation and creativity in everyday matters. This is because the knowingness which arises deep within has already scanned areas of the unknown which we as individuals are not aware of, and has taken in all of the unknown factors to synthesise these elements in order to reach an answer. If appropriate, align your divine spark with your own moral, ethical or religious allegiance, so that there is no need to compromise your integrity in any shape or form as you move forward. The best knowledge workers use not only their skill in evaluating the best options within the decision-making process but also their intuition and gut feelings when making decisions. This type of greater knowledge and awareness at the individual level is power, and being awake to these possibilities enables knowledge workers to take into account intangible knowledge so that they may ultimately differentiate themselves as outstanding workers, rather than remaining mediocre in the business environment.

Tuning into feelings and heart

As we move to the inner 'listening knowing' aspect of emotional tacit knowledge, we are able to exploit another part of the knowing process. We need to explore that part of ourselves which enables us to feel our hearts, and to 'feel' our way through life. This is the inner aspect of our individual selves. Our feelings tell us whether a person is a friend, ally, or an enemy. You may find you immediately know this intuitively. Many times we take note of the way we feel when we meet someone new and we make an instant decision. What is important in life is to listen to the inner self and to the heart, so we can align our actions to the way we feel (right feeling). Nonaka and Takeuchi (1995) in their work on knowledge creation mention 'emotional' forms of tacit knowledge but rarely give examples of what they mean by this. With a focus on the integration of mind and body, this element seems to be particularly important and needs to be further examined. Daniel Goleman's ground-breaking work on emotional intelligence includes emotional self-awareness as part of IQ. Goleman's (1996) five-dimensional framework includes self-awareness and this includes: emotional awareness; accurate self-assessment; self-confidence. Attunement to feelings offers us crucial information for navigating through life (Goleman 1996). Added to this, within the field of psychology the positive psychologists have emerged in the 1990s with the biggest paradigm shift to occur in the past 100 years. Seligman (2004) has led the way with ground-breaking work and Professor Barbara Fredrickson has provided an explanation for the role of positive emotion. Her work is known as 'the broaden and build theory of positive emotion'. The positive affect – positive emotions, positive moods and positive attitudes – may in fact be the single most important active ingredient in the recipe for human flourishing (Fredrickson 2011). Fredrickson suggests that by design, negativity inspires you to protect yourself, which often means pulling back and separating yourself from others while by design, positivity tells you it is safe to recognise that you are not separate after all.

Start today, by 'listening' to how you really feel about the direction you are going in, and the decisions you are making in life. As you lean towards joy, you are heading in the right direction. Therefore, an awareness of the negative or positive aspects of the feelings around the decisions you are making enables you to make an aware choice relating to whether or not you are in alignment with your own true nature. What we are saying here is that to get in touch with your personal knowledge you need to get in touch with your inner self (your interior, Polanyi 1966), and become aware of the way you 'feel' about the choices you make (emotional tacit knowledge creation). This also means releasing your 'ego' (release the 'ego-holic') within you so that you sidestep it, in order to listen to your own true feelings. Rather than support only the mechanical side of the brain that analyses the learned behaviour from the past, you turn to a deep inner knowing within the heart and gut to allow you to focus on the present. Your mind may tell you: 'this can't be right because it's not logical'. It may not be logical, but it is your intuition, because what you are tuning in to is your own personal 'guide' which is right for you. Therefore, link to this softer and intuitive side. Balancing the two sides is a crucial skill unless we are going to become predominantly mechanistic creatures. If not, we need to listen to the one instrument that we have been given that makes us human, and that instrument is the heart. Living with the heart really means tuning in to our feelings. Personal knowledge capital focuses on the intuitive side of our individual nature, and enables us to take greater responsibility for the decisions we make.

Personal knowledge capital is about developing yourself personally. People travel around the world to India, Tibet, and various other areas to find 'the truth'. The elusive truth! What is this truth? Why am I here? What is my purpose in life? What is it that the old sages knew, that I don't know? So we jump on a plane to go to India to search for this truth. Many people have taken this path. The truth is that you may not find the answers there at all, and the invincible truth is as simple as 'live your joy'. If you live with a 'joyful heart', then you don't need to go searching for anything. Why is no one telling us about the inner essence of our own true nature? To live your joy you have to dispel fear – fear of not daring, fear of living, and fear of life itself, as you once again take hold of your life with a bold heart, for the heartfelt journey ahead. All it takes is to let go of other people's desires for you, and be true to your own inner nature and self. To do this you need to go within.

If you develop the skill of 'listening to how you feel' in the smaller decisions you make as part of your 'listening know-how' then you have created good habits for the bigger decisions when they arise. Goleman (1996) stresses that emotional awareness starts with attunement to the stream of feelings that is a constant presence in all of us and with a recognition of how these emotions shape what we perceive, think and do. Ask yourself: Is this a good feeling or a negative feeling? If you begin to feel negative, then let go. It's not for you. You are going against yourself. Go with the flow of the good feelings. The contrast between the two is obvious (for a simple explanation see Figure 3.1). You either feel joy, love, happiness, appreciation, or you begin to feel negative with depression, despair, fear and grief. Either you allow or you resist your true feelings. Your feelings arise from your heart and gut and they are your 'guide'. Your own internal guidance system has been with you from birth, so now is the time to use it. Your deepest desires are linked to your heart and feelings, so the more deeply you feel a desire for your goals, the greater are the chances of the match occurring. Therefore, carefully match your goals, desires and target to your very deepest, deepest heart's desire.

For instance, take an example of a friend of mine who was invited to take up a new job and jumped at the chance, thinking this was a great opportunity. When they got to their destination the doubts began to creep in, as it was not quite what they expected. It wasn't long before their gut told them that they were not gelling with the group they were allocated to look after or the situation they found themselves in. On weighing up the situation they decided to leave the post. What was interesting about this was that they noted on departure that they felt a great sigh of relief, and a lifting of spirit. This job was not right for them, for whatever reason. The sigh of relief was telling them just that. Learning to identify the signs in terms of your awareness of how you feel

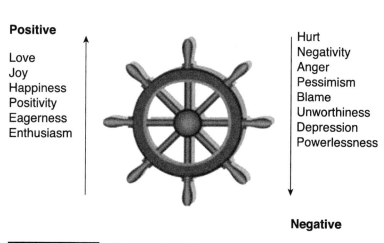

Positive

Love
Joy
Happiness
Positivity
Eagerness
Enthusiasm

Hurt
Negativity
Anger
Pessimism
Blame
Unworthiness
Depression
Powerlessness

Negative

Figure 3.1   The emotional scale
Image used with permission from Microsoft

(such as being aware of the 'sigh' and lifting of spirits) is important because then you are awake enough to understand what is true for you. Be alert to your 'feelings', and how you react to situations as they arise.

Stop and take a moment to check out your inner emotional scale (Figure 3.1), and the thoughts that are linked to how you feel about a situation or decision. When did you last relate significantly to one or the other side of the scales? Once you have set in motion what you want, then allow it to be, let it in, in order to lessen the resistance that you have at a deep level. Examine and feel your own resistance to what it is you actually want. Where does it arise on a scale of 1 to 10? If the resistance is high, why have you got your foot on the brakes? This practice may help you identify why you are resisting, so that you can work on being open to new opportunities as they present themselves. Creating awareness and tuning into your emotions enables you to ask what is this feeling telling me? What is the intention behind it? By doing this you are tuning in to your own inner guidance system (your 'inner know-how' as part of emotional tacit knowledge creation) in order to listen for solutions and prompts in whatever shape or form they may arise.

Zen: quiet time for creativity (the tools for personal knowledge)

Quiet time is the elixir of life for creativity! Creative solutions are at the heart of inspirational thinking, and have great intangible value. We all want to be creative, but wonder how to get there. Finding time to get into the zone where creative ideas flow and inspire us, in an exciting place to be. Personal knowledge capital at the individual level is all about encouraging yourself to 'go within'. This means carefully listening to the still small silent voice that may arise within the interior of our being. In other words you need to allow yourself some Zen time. Your inner voice is the 'real you'. So how do we proceed to do this? The first step is to take time out to be very quiet. What you are looking for is quiet time with yourself. This may mean going for a long walk with the dog; walking for miles along the beach or in the countryside, or it may mean you loose yourself by painting or simply walking in a beautiful landscape. An example is a friend who hears songs when she relaxes and walks in the countryside or along the coast, and the songs help her to hear her inner voice, and understand the problem and solution. She then reflects on the message, and understands the answer to the problem. Loosing yourself in this simple way is a way of reaching your inner core. It may be that you do Tai-chi or an equivalent in order to loose yourself and find the inner space and silence that leads to the inner spark. Of course, another route and more constructive way of doing this could be through meditation. As stressed, as part of the integration of mind–body experiences, Nonaka and Takeuchi (1995) highlight that the tradition of emphasising bodily experiences through body and mind is the ultimate ideal condition that Zen practitioners seek by means of internal meditation and disciplined life. Meditation is a way of reaching into the still silent space and is a mechanism for reaching personal experience over external experiences. Regular usage of this process may lead to synchronistic occurrences and signs occurring to show you the way. You do need to commit to regular 'quiet time' with yourself, in order to be effective, and reap the benefits from listening to the 'inner guru'. This method may involve a pre-planned regular 30-minute meditation twice a day. Early in the morning and late in the afternoon is desirable. Having spent some time in a quiet space in silence meditating, you may wish to complete the session by carefully asking for answers and creative solutions. Allow the inner silence in the quiet space, and listen for the answers and ask for creative solutions. Pre-prepare and plan for quiet time and spend time in your space, then focus on your dilemma or question. After you have done this, listen to the inner prompts or creative solutions that may spontaneously arise. Allow your own inner self to help guide you by aligning to your own 'internal guidance system' and internal wisdom. Create the future you want through your own personal knowledge capital so that you become the master. Do this by looking within to the essence of your being, rather than looking without for answers.

To be creative you need to create quiet space within and around yourself. This peaceful space then allows your inner creative nature to expand and present meaningful and unique solutions to problems and issues. In other words, spending time with yourself in this way enables you to block out some of the constant noise that we receive, and makes way for new ideas to emerge. As discussed, a variety of techniques are available to do this. If you create a quiet space in the silence, you will find that creative solutions come to mind. This happens when you allow yourself quiet time. This type of access to knowledge can be useful and enable the knowledge worker to add to, and complement, corporate information. To find answers you need to go within to listen to your own 'listening know-how' as part of your 'personal knowledge capital'. Thus your own personal knowledge capital system allows you to maximise your full potential to become the real you, and in doing so tap into the reserve of emotional tacit knowledge and 'know-how' that resides within yourself. Therefore, solutions may be intuitive as well as rational for the knowledge worker. Indeed, Nonaka and Takeuchi (1995) emphasise the need to bring about continuous innovation through the linkage between the outside and the inside.

Appreciating different forms of tacit knowledge including emotional knowledge assets and know-how becomes imperative for the organisation. As already discussed, Nonaka's work on the tacit dimension enables an understanding of the process, but the SECI model does not delve deeply into what is meant by 'know-how' or intuitive tacit knowledge at the individual, let alone collective level within the SECI model of knowledge creation. In this respect, Nonaka's SECI model can appear to lack depth in its explanation of knowledge creation. The first part of the process is listening within in order to fine-tune to our own feelings and find a Zen space to practise 'listening know-how'. In this way, tuning in and listening to the interior can put you in charge of your personal knowledge capital. The daily practices explored are mechanisms and tools to help you fully explore the inner tacit knowledge available to you and tap into its creative and innovative solutions and self-mastery.

Summary

We have stated that listening to the inner spark and using this intuitive level (your inner guidance system) enables knowledge workers to make use of all aspects of themselves and helps to complement rational business solutions with inspiring creative solutions. These areas of knowingness and personal awareness may be acknowledged as part of 'emotional tacit knowledge' in knowledge creation and can be valued by both the individual knowledge worker and the collective group within the organisation. An awareness of the means to acquire 'emotional tacit knowledge' is important for bringing about change and creative solutions in organisations in order to appreciate its impact on the individual and collective level. In this way know-how at the individual level develops, and this could lead to creating greater individual and corporate level creativity and innovation.

Reflective exercises

1. Think back to how many times you just knew about something about to arise in your stirrings in the 'heart and gut'.

   What did it feel like?

   Did you take note?

   Did you react and listen at the time, or did you ignore this sensation?

2. Do you take time out to spend quiet time with yourself?

   Do you take time out each day to listen to your own inner quiet voice?

3. What role does your own personal deep layer of 'know-how' play in your current personal and professional working life today?

4. Spend time relaxing. This could be outdoors or indoors, walking in the countryside, relaxing, painting or listening to meditation tapes. Any or all of these methods can be used if it helps to still the chatty mind. Find a space where you are going to be completely quiet, alone and comfortable. Then after a period of deep quiet and silence, ask the questions you want answered. Listen attentively and catch the answers, solutions and clues to your questions. To be effective you need to do this regularly and make it practice and habit.

(Wait for the answers and solutions, and record your success when it does occur. In this way by recording your success you can build on it to access your emotional tacit knowledge!)

Creating quiet time for meditation: Example

One way of using meditation is by using primordial meditation where a mantra (string of words) is used. Deepak Chopra recommends primordial meditation. This involves constantly repeating the mantra over and over, so that you loose your thoughts and get nearer to your inner being. The words have a vibrational quality about them and this takes you closer to your inner world. It is all about getting into alignment with your real self and inner being in order to connect to the real you. This is a tool and a mechanism for getting in touch with yourselves. Some people use stillness or mindfulness as a method, alternatively others use guided meditation CDs. Whatever method you use, quiet time helps you focus with the intention of finding the answer/solution. Your own inner 'knowing' will guide you. After some time in this quiet inner space you have created for yourself, you can set your intentions for the future. You need to practise your own quiet time every day, and commit to this practice without compromise. Find time in your daily routine when this can be achieved by project managing your day-to-day practice. Ask the questions you wish to have answered, and listen intently for the solutions. Of course, you need to take time to formulate your personal goals/intentions or work-related issues. This may mean carefully considering the direction in which you wish your daily

---

life events to go. Small goals are always stepping stones to moving forward in the right direction. Fully explore the goals that you specifically want to achieve (be sure it feels right – rightness) before embarking on activity (Exercise 4 above). The skill of listening in quiet space has to be developed and practised.

5. Do you let your 'know-how' influence your business activity? Why or why not? Are you spending time in your quiet space to 'feel and sense' what you consider to be right? Do you feel good about it? Does it feel right? Does it feel negative? What are these feeling processes telling you?

4

Mastering self
and behaviour

Abstract: How do you master the individual cognitive processes in order to harness your own power? This chapter examines what steps the knowledge worker can take to process their cognitive personal knowledge creation to ultimately gain control in a variety of work environments. Mastering thoughts and reflecting on behaviour enables new insights to arise.

Key words: personal knowledge creation, self-mastery and inner personal knowledge capital, behavioural capital.

So far we have emphasised that in personal knowledge capital we need to go within to find our knowledge. As part of this process it would seem imperative to carefully evaluate our thought patterns. Are they positive or negative? This is a starting point in helping you reach self-mastery. Knowledge starts with the individual in knowledge creation and because of this we need to examine tacit knowledge in more detail. We have already discussed the cognitive dimension of tacit knowledge sharing in Chapter 1. In order to expand the cognitive dimension of knowledge creation, the focus will be on the self-evaluation of our own thoughts in an endeavour to look at thought management.

The power of thought

With inner personal knowledge capital we must carefully observe our own 'self talk', or in other words our thoughts. This may also be called the 'mind print', where the process of an imprint being made on your mind has a very powerful effect (Roach 2000). Ryde (2007) uses the analogy of a raindrop to the movement and direction of our thinking. He suggests that we may be pulled by the path already taken by previous raindrops and we may get stuck in this channel of thinking. Ryde suggests that we may work to review the roots of the thinking styles to enable self-awareness, and suggests six dominant thinking styles: deficit; rational; common-sense; equity; binary and sticky. Interestingly, the shadow opposite of rational turns into feeling thinking where, for instance, we might ask what does our gut instinct tell us about this situation? However, in terms of self-awareness the point here is that awareness of thoughts can be a small first step to making changes and shaping thinking.

Observing your own thoughts is the first step to redesigning your future. Reflecting on your thoughts makes you aware of the way that you are thinking. Ask yourself: Is the language used in my thoughts (your self-talk) predominantly negative or positive? What sort of language am I using? Take note. Can you hear yourself say sentences like 'I am not good at . . .'? If you keep repeating this negative phrase then soon it will turn into action. So make sure you turn it around so that this becomes: 'I am in the process of creating good relationships', or 'I am in the process of working on this situation . . .' or 'I am in the process of finding a new job'. Now the self-talk is more positive, so rather than continuing with the negative talk, turn it around to say in your head 'I am in the process of . . .'. Watch and observe the self-talk that keeps re-occurring in your mind and make a list of the

46

negative so you can work on it. Then turn the negative language in your mind around into positive self-talk, which will guide you to be in a more peaceful, positive space and restful direction. Don't drown in the sea of your own negativity, when you can float on the ocean of life (Hay 1991). In this way, you become the master, rather than being subservient to your thoughts. What you think attracts more of what you think; therefore, pay attention to what you think about. All this suggests that we should be careful about what we think, as it leads to what we create and forms part of our cognitive tacit knowledge creation.

Pruning the garden of your mind

If we can keep a careful check on our mind then it will reap rewards in terms of enabling us to go in the direction that we wish to pursue. Sharma (2008) emphasises that if you care for your mind, if you nurture it, and if you cultivate it just like a fertile rich garden, it will blossom far beyond your expectations. He suggests that if you let the weeds take root, lasting peace of mind and deep inner harmony will elude you, as toxic weeds are toxic thoughts. Therefore, think about the toxic waste in the 'fertile' garden of the mind (Sharma 2008). Sharma also suggests that when an undesirable thought occupies the focal point of your mind you should immediately replace it with an uplifting one.

Mental mastery and thought management are important for the individual knowledge worker because we need to take responsibility for what we cultivate while we stand guard at the gate of our own personal garden. This is in an extension of the cognitive dimension of tacit knowledge creation. Watch how you think and react to situations, especially in the workplace. If our thoughts are formed by our mental imprints and are part of our personal knowledge, we owe it to ourselves to watch how we react to situations. In other words, when the going gets tough – start watching your thought patterns! For example, a friend of mine waited three years for a new apartment to be built in their favourite spot. After all the various delays, the agent offers to take them around to do some early snagging. A great opportunity! Arriving at the apartment with the agent they found that the apartment was in a bad way after a rainstorm. Shock overwhelmed them. The tears came to the fore. Are you observing? Well, yes, but how about viewing the situation in a different light? What about saying thank you for highlighting this to me, before I have paid the final part of the deposit, which is twice as much as I have already put down. Did they really want to invest in a property that had these problems without knowing about it? It is the way you view the situation that is important. You can view this through a positive or negative lens. In the long term, awareness of this situation can only be for the good and you have managed to see the real issue. Now you can do something about it. Maybe there is an alternative, or you can walk away. A good idea would be to give thanks for having had this pointed out to you, and suggest a creative solution for the money already invested. Whatever the outcome, actually this was a good day, not a bad day. This is an example of initially viewing a negative situation from a more positive point of view. Watch your thoughts! How are you proceeding with this? Are your initial thoughts reality or perception? Can you change the way you think about a situation, in order to change the outcome? If you can do this then you become the master of your own change. By using this mechanism you become the master of your thoughts in order to maintain a positive attitude and outcome. In this way, the knowledge worker can positively move forward in the workplace.

The emotional wheel

Start using the process above to make the changes and drive your own future. Building on the emotional scale in Figure 3.1, use the idea of visualising in your mind a wheel, which you can use to place your thoughts and their link to feelings on a range from very positive to very negative. This way you can quickly evaluate your current state: how happy, or not, are you really feeling according to your thoughts? Visualise the wheel in your mind, and try to map your thoughts on the wheel. If your thoughts are very negative, create new ones that will allow you to move to the next level on the wheel. A gentle move forward! Let's take an example of how this works. Supposing you go for a job interview, or for a verbal examination – in both instances someone, in effect, is evaluating you and examining your verbal abilities. In this process you are quiet and nervous, and feel very overpowered as there are a number of panel members evaluating you. The outcome of this process is that you are not offered the job. The real point here is how you react to this news. What immediately comes to mind? What are the mental models within the mind (or mental footprint) you are creating? For many of us it would be: 'I'm not good enough', or 'I can't possibly succeed in the future'. In terms of work prospects, you feel deep elements of despair, alienation and hurt. However, despite your despair at this news, if you are able to evaluate the situation and re-evaluate your own self-worth by reflecting on your own thoughts and mental footprints, then you can take charge and repair this situation by re-assessing it in terms of potential lack of fit between the job and the real you. By staying positive you can look forward to, and embrace, the idea of a better post in the future.

In terms of the power of thought, you can use your internal visualisation process to picture the wheel, assess where you are, and try to move one step forward on the wheel. Once you have taken charge of the outcome, you create your own reality rather than let others do so. If you let others do this, then you become the victim of other people's varying perceptions of reality. When you take charge, other people's perceptions cannot influence your reality. Once again, you become the master of your own destiny. Therefore, keep a close eye on your thoughts, and reflect on a regular basis on your own 'mental footprint' in order to note where your thoughts might lead you. This is the first step that eventually becomes part of your own personal knowledge creation, self-mastery and inner personal knowledge capital. This process can be viewed as part of your 'cognitive self-mastery' in knowledge creation terms.

Think, feel and behave

So far, we have talked about being awake to mastering our own thoughts, in order to observe how we think. Cope (2000) asks: 'Are we open to new ways of viewing the world, or are we closed minded to new ideas'? Cope argues that how we think, feel and behave (along with using terminology such as head, hand and heart) all come together to form our personal capital or private assets that allow us to trade our knowledge in the market. If we take Cope's comments about how we think, feel and behave we realise that our thoughts, mental models (ways of viewing the world) and behaviour all form part of our personal knowledge. In this way, our feelings about a person or culture become part of our personal capital. Cope suggests that some people spread rumours or gossip, and that they may think they have knowledge, which in fact turns out to be false! This behaviour could eventually backfire and devalue their personal knowledge commodity. This, coupled with unintentional poor social skills, may lead to the devaluing of your personal knowledge. Cope's ideas all link to valuing personal knowledge, private assets, and ways of trading and communicating these assets to the outside world. You cannot do this unless you are able to specifically identify your own unique assets, and then place value on them.

Let's take an example of how you think and view the world. How do you react when as a highly respected professional you take up a new international post, for which you have been given a high level of responsibility? The director tells you within a few days of taking up the post that you must not leave your housing compound to conduct research. In your own culture you are valued and respected, but in this context you feel degraded because you are not being allowed a driver to leave the housing compound where you live. You have not learned to drive on the other side of the road yet – so ultimately you have been placed under house arrest! The normal reaction for the professional is to strike out and resign from the job on the spot, and be totally outraged. However, perhaps on reflection in a calmer mood you wonder whether this is part of the culture to which you have signed up, and whether your current lack of cultural awareness is part of the learning process. Upon reflection you are more attuned to this position, but still do not condone the principle.

It is all part of the way that you think, and the way that you think varies in and between cultures. We should take into account that what is acceptable practice in one culture/society is not acceptable in another. As you have never experienced this before, feeling a sense of outrage goes along with your cultural upbringing, and is a normal reaction. Behaving in this manner also fits into the category of 'behavioural personal capital', which may be generated from the culture you belong to, and becomes another element within personal knowledge capital. This type of sensitive awareness of cultural differences and gender tolerance (provided by awareness of your behavioural personal capital) only comes with time, practice and life experiences. However, the personal capital gained from it is also part of the learning experience. Whether these experiences are the norm within a professional environment in some parts of the world may vary, depending on how enlightened the players are within the scenario in which you are operating.

Summary

In this chapter we have discussed observing and watching thought patterns and being aware of what we create. Mastering the above individual cognitive inner processes gives you power to move forward into a place where you wish to reside rather than be the victim of circumstances. This area of thinking self-awareness enables us to shape our own positive thinking patterns rather than slip back into negative patterns. The emotional wheel is a tool and a visualisation mechanism to help you move forward. This approach forms part of the tuning-in process viewed as 'cognitive self-mastery' and can be regarded as part of the cognitive dimension of tacit knowledge within knowledge creation. In particular, personal knowledge is still an area that is developing and the dimensions of individual cognitive and technical tacitness include 'emotional know-how'.

Reflective self-assessment questions

1. Create your own future by being self-aware and examining the thoughts you are creating. Be aware of the

mental footprints, your thoughts. When you find a negative mental footprint, can you change it into a positive one?

2. Can you think of a negative scenario? Re-enact the situation that was caused by your current situation? Can you replay this scene in your head so that you can re-enact it from different perspectives until you reach a more positive viewpoint?

3. How can you replace negative thoughts with positive thought processes in the corporate environment to achieve your goals, and re-evaluate your 'personal behavioural capital'?

5

Ka, the knowledge awareness model for knowledge creation

Abstract: Sometimes a visual model helps you to remember a process that you can use to develop your awareness. This chapter will help you do just that. Building on the discussion in Chapters 2, 3 and 4, this chapter draws together all the previous discussions to create a new model and thereby extend the SECI model of knowledge creation to include a model for personal knowledge awareness.

Key words: Ka, Co-Ka, the knowledge awareness representation, The inner path of knowledge creation, the LOFT model.

In Chapter 2 we identified that 'knowingness' was an underdeveloped concept in Nonaka's knowledge creation theory, and in Chapter 3 we examined this element in greater detail as a sensing emotional knowledge that can be utilised. Then in Chapter 4 we focused on the development of the inner cognitive abilities to master thoughts. In this way the development of the inner openness of the mind–body association is acknowledged. Chapter 5 endeavours to develop Nonaka, Toyama and Konno's (2000) Unified Model of Knowledge Creation into the Accessible Awareness Model of Knowledge Creation.

Developing knowingness

Having an awareness of the value of inner knowledge within individuals in the organisation may enable organisations to achieve greater intangible value in the future. Despite knowing and know-how being a fuzzy area to define, it lends itself to being an area where there could be transformational change within the organisation. As discussed in Chapter 1, enlightened knowledge workers and leaders who are focused on the development of personal knowing could find their know-how expanding collectively outwards to the group level. In this sense knowing, instinct, gut feel, and hidden intelligence may be defined as part of an individual's inner spark. Acknowledging and listening to this level of awareness and knowing may enable access to greater levels of guidance for the individual to support both individual and collective innovation and creativity. Through intuition, this individual 'knowing' then spirals outwards into the organisation to the collective group level. Senge, Scharmer, Jaworski and Flowers (2005) highlight the importance of embracing and mobilising 'tacit knowledge and knowing' at the collective level within the corporate organisation in order to transform and encourage deep change and innovation. Comprehending the subtleties in this subconscious area of individual personal knowledge is important in order to appreciate the impact at the individual and collective level in the organisation.

Ka: the knowledge awareness model of knowledge creation

While Nonaka et al. (2000) added three new dimensions to the original SECI model (including ba, a time space nexus;

knowledge creation assets and leadership management), the proposal here is to develop the representation further by introducing the concept of Ka which focuses on the internal personal knowledge – awareness – know-how – intelligence which the knowledge worker may access. The Ka acronym means K for knowledge and A for awareness and accessibility internal to the knowledge worker. The Ka arises and develops the unified model itself, interlinking at a deeper level to the socialisation and internalisation processes. Ka is the knowledge, the know-how and the wisdom that resides within the individual, which can be accessed and sensed in order to gain a new quality of understanding by being aware of awareness itself at the inner level. Ka arises from the individual's ability to listen to the interior, sensing, scanning, feeling, tuning in to the heart and gut within to achieve an expansiveness into knowingness which links to a greater truth (inner wisdom). Being in touch by going within enables the individual to be aware of another creative dimension and a skill set which is available to them at short notice. It enables them to be open to the boundless possibilities of the infinite intelligence. The new representation and framework would then look like the following:

Ka: Deeply delving into personal inner knowledge capital through sensing know-how and awareness of thoughts at the individual level.

Socialisation: Sharing of experiences between individuals.

Externalisation: Articulating tacit knowledge into explicit concepts.

Combination: Systemising concepts into a knowledge system (combining different bodies of explicit knowledge).

Internalisation: Embodying explicit knowledge into tacit knowledge (learning by doing).

The LOFT

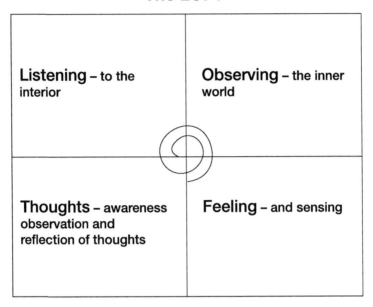

Listening – to the interior	**Observing** – the inner world
Thoughts – awareness observation and reflection of thoughts	**Feeling** – and sensing

Figure 5.1 'Ka', the knowledge awareness model of knowledge creation incorporates the LOFT

The LOFT forms part of the knowledge awareness model and can be gainfully employed to bring personal knowledge capital to the fore, by acting as a reminder of the processes that can be used for personal development. In Figure 5.1 and Table 5.1 the Ka is broken down into four further elements which start with the individual knowledge worker's ability to first (L) listen and go to a quiet space within themselves to listen to their own 'know-how' residing within the body. This enables the knowledge worker to feel their way into a situation or decision by listening to the interior knowledge that already exists, and is just waiting to be accessed. This process includes listening to the quiet voice of the inner heart, and it eventually leads to a greater awareness of the wisdom of the intelligence within. Secondly, (O) is for observing and sensing. Attentive observation is required to catch the inner voice. Thirdly, the knowledge worker moves to (F) the feeling and sensing part of themselves, keeping a strong sense of awareness as to whether the feelings are positive, negative or neutral. Observe, assess and examine the feeling to find out why you have it. Accept the feeling, and then work to move it forward if negative. Fourthly (T) involves an awareness of thoughts and self-talk, and can prompt a reflection on how positive thoughts might be. Here, the knowledge worker can look for the source of the thought to attain the emotion linked to the negative thought and thereby acknowledge this, move on or try to change the thought by taking a step forward to a more positive place. This leads to self-mastery. Through this process the knowledge worker is pruning the mind to take full control and responsibility for his/her outcomes. The LOFT model encompasses listening, sensing, feeling and observing thoughts to achieve stillness, intuitive wisdom and self-mastery. The process enables a spiral of knowledge interacting within all four elements. The outcome of the above is that the knowledge worker experiences knowingness and wisdom from within the heart - an interior place of deep inner wisdom. The LOFT forms part of feeling and sensing within emotional tacit knowledge; it links to emotional tacit knowledge assets and forms part of cognitive tacit knowledge. The author proposes that the original model by Nonaka, Toyama and Konno (2000) be extended to take into account the development of the 'Ka' individual know-how and how it links to the SECI model, which will enable a deeper understanding of the unconscious knowledge that exists within the knowledge worker which is accessible when tuned into (see Figure 5.2).

Ka within the Knowledge Awareness representation (Figure 5.2) includes six levels for knowledge creation:

- SECI (Knowledge creation processes)
- Ka (Inner accessibility and awareness for individual personal knowledge)

Table 5.1	The LOFT: inner individual knowledge for personal knowledge capital

THE LOFT	
Listening	**Go within and spend quiet time with yourself.** Listen to the inner voice and wisdom within the interior silence.
Observing	**Sense, observe and listen.** Observe mindfully what you sense. Attentive listening is required. Sense and catch meaning within this space.
Feelings	**Feel it. Listen to the heart. Feelings relate to the heart.** Sense, assess the meaning of the feeling. Does it feel positive? What does it feel like?
Thoughts	**Watch your thoughts. Observation of thoughts leads to self-mastery.** Be aware and observe and reflect on thoughts: are they positive or negative or neutral? Awareness leads to changes, acceptance, questioning and looking for the feeling associated with thought? The why? Move to a place where you can change negative unpleasant thinking place into a positive thought. Ask why am I allowing myself to think like this? Become the gardener of your own self-talk.
Knowingness: The spiral creates the energy over time as we consistently manage the LOFT in our own internal space. Deep inner knowing links to inner wisdom, the heart wisdom and spiritual spark and leads to wakefulness, awareness and divine consciousnesses (greater self).	

Source: Young (2011)

- KCA (Knowledge Creation Assets)
- Ba (Time and space nexus)
- Management (Generate vision – facilitate and direct)
- Co-Ka (To be developed with groups and teams over time).

In Figure 5.2 each part of the figure is labelled to explain the adapted Unified Model of Knowledge Creation to include Ka. The Unifed Model of Knowledge Creation is fully discussed later, in Chapter 11. The following is a brief overview and representation to give an idea of how Ka

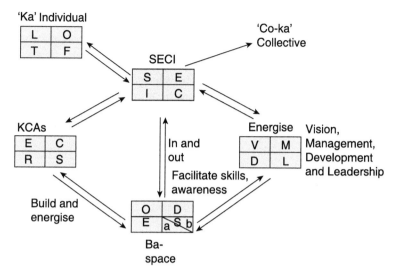

'Ka' Individual

'Co-ka' Collective

SECI

KCAs

In and out

Energise   Vision, Management, Development and Leadership

Facilitate skills, awareness

Build and energise

Ba-space

Figure 5.2   The knowledge awareness representation of Ka

and Co-Ka relate to the model where SECI involves S) socialisation, E) externalisation, I) internalisation and C) combination. The SECI is the starting point and the heart of the model of knowledge creation. The Knowledge Creation Assets (KCAs) include E) experiential, C) conceptual, R) routine and S) systemic. The interactions of the two parts occur as inputs and outputs in the knowledge creation process. The Ba includes the O) originating, D) dialogue (albeit physical), E) exercising and S) systemising (where the systemising is sub-divided in to the interactive and the systemising element within a virtual space). The Ka occurs at a deeper level with the socialisation process within the SECI model and at a deeper level links to experiential Knowledge Creation Assets. The Ka is sub-divided into L) listening, O) observation F) feelings and T) thoughts and stands for know-how, knowledge, infinite intelligence and wisdom, and this is represented in the spiral. A Co-Ka element has been placed in Figure 5.2 for future thought and this relates to the

Ka being collectively shared in groups with other Co-Ka workers. The arrows represent the flow in and around the SECI. The Accessible Model of Knowledge Creation delves deeply into know-how to make knowledge creation accessible from the inner interior of the knowledge worker so they can access their inner wisdom.

From 'Ka' inner knowledge to 'Co-Ka' presencing

The introduction of the 'Ka' into the knowledge creation model means that intuitive individual know-how is acknowledged as being of value within the organisation. Thus 'Ka' forms part of individual presencing that arises inside the knowledge worker. The 'Ka' may then be brought into dialogue and conversation with other members of the organisation at the collective group level to become part of a collective presencing (Co-Ka) which, when valued, becomes powerful at this level. Collective Ka is a powerful tool to be utilised in the work environment. If all the players are indeed linking to their inner Ka, and also cooperating, they may focus on an intent or solution by using these processes to produce collaborative Ka, which can be very powerful in the workplace.

Although knowing is a fuzzy area to define, it lends itself to being an area where there could be transformational change within the organisation. Enlightened leadership focusing on the development of personal knowing could even be expanded outwards to the group level. In this sense, knowing, instinct, gut feel and 'hidden intelligence' as part of inner wisdom may form part of an individual's personal self-awareness. In other words, through intuition the individual knowing then spirals outwards in the organisation to the collective group level (called Co-Ka), and may eventually lead to innovative solutions through corporate cooperative presencing (Co-Ka). Senge, Scharmer, Jaworski and Flowers (2005) discuss this collective concept, calling it presencing. They highlight the importance of embracing and mobilising 'tacit knowledge and knowing' at the collective level within the corporate organisation in order to transform and encourage deep change and innovation. Understanding the subtleties in this subconscious area of individual personal knowledge is important to understanding the theory in order to appreciate the impact on the collective level in the organisation. If we go deep, there is both a collective knowing, where those involved use the know-how and intuition (Ka) to make collective presencing for corporate decision-making, and there is collective decision-making that is non-intuitive. While some individuals may be using this process to complement decision-making, others may not, and this needs to be clearly understood. There needs to be an awareness of whether you are working with collective Ka or with individuals who are not using their inner know-how.

In particular, the development of framework (Figure 5.2) is a means by which greater levels of intuitive know-how can be accessed by the knowledge workers and leaders so that decisions and directions do not have to fall entirely within the remit of a mechanical research and scanning process. By using this approach, knowledge workers can use a type of intuitive knowledge in the form of 'Ka' not only for their own personal development but collectively for their own organisation. They can, in fact, complement the mechanical processes that are presented by twentieth-century management practice by using intangible knowledge in the process, thereby interacting in the new twenty-first-century management paradigm. When this type of activity is acknowledged and accepted within organisations, leaders will have begun to tune into the intangible as well as the tangible elements available to them. It has been said that the most successful leaders use their intuitive abilities, and in practice this model helps the knowledge worker to achieve this through being fully aware of the process and techniques to do so.

By introducing Ka we are saying that the knowledge worker at the organisational level can go within to use their own inner intelligence to find 'Ka', and to make effective outputs, sense the right direction to travel, and address the lack and limitations of an approach that until now has been focused on an external reality and mechanical ways of gleaning information to inform choice. There is, therefore, an emphasis on the knowledge worker using intuitive know-how to complement rational processes. The hope is that these ideas and concepts will become the norm in future organisations and that it will be considered acceptable practice for management to value intangible insights derived from the knowledge worker's inner reference system so that this element may be valued and accepted as part of organisational practices.

Summary

A worker's ability to tap into his/her own inner core knowledge enables them to use individual know-how in the form of cognitive sensing and listening sensing as well as using analytical processes to make decisions. The best knowledge workers are those who have an awareness of this inner know-how, and in other words use their own inner wisdom or personal knowledge capital to transform situations and make decisions using their higher level of consciousness. We have already discussed how this deep level of knowing and know-how arising at the individual level was not fully addressed within Nonaka's SECI model, and that exploration of this subconscious level takes us into the realm of knowing that is the focus of this chapter. The reason for this may be that Nonaka did not want to delve into spiritual, cognitive and psychological aspects of individual knowledge and knowing, and he has therefore limited the boundaries in advance. The SECI model may have limitations for those wishing to explore the individual cognitive and deeper elements of tacit knowledge in more depth. The author proposes that Nonaka, Toyama and Konno's (2000) unified model be extended into the realms of personal knowledge capital as discussed above in order to expand the capacity of the knowledge worker by entering into the individual's own inner personal knowledge known as 'Ka'. Therefore, the representation (Knowledge Awareness Access Model, Figure 5.2) develops from the SECI and unified model. The 'Ka' arises at the deepest level of socialisation and internalisation with the SECI model and becomes another part of the model relating to an individual's personal knowledge capital. We have extended the Unified Model of Knowledge Creation by adapting the representation for a greater fit, by adding a new dimension of 'Ka' for greater levels of creativity and innovation. Appreciating different forms of tacit knowledge, emotional tacit knowledge and knowing as part of knowledge creation theory will become imperative for organisations in the future.

Reflective exercises

1. What is 'Ka' and why is it important to the knowledge worker in the twenty-first-century organisation? How does it fit into a twenty-first-century management paradigm?

2. What can the 'Ka' process contribute in the field of knowledge creation? How can 'Ka' become a useful approach for the business professional?

3. What does 'collective Ka' (Co-Ka) really mean? How can 'Co-Ka' create greater value for the organisation?

Part 2

The outer path of personal knowledge capital in a web environment

Image used with permission from Microsoft

'Today, we have to look with new eyes at the mystery of existence, for as proud children of science and reason, we have made ourselves the orphans of wisdom.' Chopra (2004)

The outer path of knowledge creation shifts our attention to how the knowledge worker communicates and collaborates in the interactive web world. The outer path explores community, culture, social capital, relationships and trust issues when interacting in the outside world. It examines the unified theory of knowledge creation before making new suggestions for knowledge creation within a virtual world. This pathway brings forward a set of tools, models and frameworks that could be useful for designing and developing a knowledge-focused virtual environment.

6

Personal knowledge and network building

Abstract: Networking is at the heart of good business. Evaluating on a regular basis the connections of relationships you have acquired and what value to place on them is an important business skill. In knowledge terms we can value the strength of ties associated with the network, and may wish to evaluate the trust built up within these networks. Reflective practice is a tool to be used, and is at the heart of good management development and leads to continuous improvement and lessons learnt.

Key words: networks, shadow knowledge, reflective practice.

Good educational qualifications like the MBA should teach you to network effectively in order to be successful. Today, good MBA programmes teach students to place value on the intangibles such as personal knowledge and networking. Although many programmes are clearly focused on the bottom line and the hard tangible elements of business, such a narrow focus leaves little space for the human and behavioural elements wherein intangible value resides. Perhaps this is because the intangibles are, after all, far more difficult to define as they are 'sticky'. This chapter aims to look at the outer rather than inner personal knowledge by first focusing on the network of relationships we develop through which we can share and trade our information and knowledge.

The strength of a wide band of professional networks is that it gives you access to deep and tacit knowledge across a wide spectrum. In the twenty-first-century personal knowledge is all about placing value on the intangible value, inclusive of the networks you create. This means taking notice of the personal and social relationships you create and the contacts you make. In doing so, you need to think about placing value on the people in your business network, so that your network becomes part of your social capital. Cope (2003) suggests that 'who you know' generally does count for more than what you know. In other words, successful people do two things: they develop a wide span of connections, and they develop 'know what' to make these connections count. As such a personal network can act as a resource that supports ideas; opportunities; influence; access to power and goodwill. Placing value on the strength of the 'ties' within the relationships in your business network enables you to assess the value of those relationships. Some ties may be valued more highly than others, as some ties will be weak and others will be much stronger. You can work with your integrity to build up networks of trust, and network with those people that you feel good about. You can categorise your network, and connect with those you *intuitively feel in alignment* with. Of course there will always be those people who fall into the category of 'vulture-like networker'. You can see them coming, any opportunity is grabbed at visibly. Step back and reflect when you meet this type of person, before making a decision as to where to categorise them within your own network. Do you want to work with them at all? Use your integrity to make that decision.

One should value relationships and manage them. In addition, it is important to understand that people buy from people they like, and that relationships are key to business.

We all have a 'circle of influence'. At the individual level you should store and create a 'bank of good will' with your contacts. People don't like to be used so you need to be sincere. Therefore, think carefully about loyalty within the relationship. Look at the 'circle of influence' around you and weigh it up. Is it *hostile, non-supportive, neutral, supportive, or very supportive*? This may help you make judgements about the environment you find yourself working in, as it may help you assess whether you are in the right environment. Manage the relationship, not the person! Think carefully about the idea of what they need from you. It doesn't mean you lose your integrity by using these methods providing you view this in a business context. What the MBA will teach you is that you need to quickly develop the skill to hone in and become politically smart.

Good relationships and caring environments

As a knowledge worker, making best use of your contacts is important but building long-term relationships in the workplace is also imperative. Von Krogh, Ichijo and Nonaka (2000) suggest that good relationships purge a knowledge creation process of distrust, fear and dissatisfaction, and allow organisational members to feel safe enough to explore the unknown territories of new markets, customers, products and manufacturing technologies. At a more basic level, the ways in which people interact in terms of cooperative sharing versus competitive hoarding, 'join us' versus 'not at my table', may strongly affect the distribution of tacit knowledge (Von Krogh et al. 2000). Thus, the sharing of tacit knowledge requires careful nurturing. Von Krogh et al. emphasise that the hoarding of knowledge is one of the fundamental issues of modern business organisations, and they suggest that this is why the concept of care as a condition for knowledge creation has relevance for today's companies. In this respect, the extent to which organisational members feel they can openly suggest new concepts and ideas, as well as convey and receive constructive criticism without fear of reprisal, is crucial. In a caring culture, members of the organisation do not feel threatened and in this open and safe environment they begin to share, create new knowledge and generate ideas. This view is particularly relevant to knowledge sharing at the micro level within an organisation, and to the relationships people form, because these relationships influence culture.

Shadow knowledge

A note of caution: you should be aware of the shadow knowledge occurring in the organisation. Shadow knowledge is one of the unspoken problems associated with knowledge management. Cope (2000) argues that knowledge can exist in two forms. One is *surface knowledge,* which is in the public domain and open. The other is *shadow knowledge,* which is hidden from normal view. The shadow side deals with the covert; the undiscussed; the undiscussable; the unmentionable! Tension may exist in organisations between the open organisation and the hidden organisation, and the open individual and the hidden individual. In essence, companies manage the knowledge they want to see, rather than what they need to see! In this way, companies try to protect themselves from pain. Cope makes the point that 'If people don't accept their *own shadow knowledge,* then what chance is there that they will take responsibility for surfacing issues that cause problems for the business?' Cope's argument reminds us to first value people – a bottom-up approach. In the future, Cope believes that exploitation of your capability means you must learn to map, measure and market your personal capital. However, the personal knowledge capital approach as described here emphasises the importance of both 'internal knowledge' and 'external knowledge', where internal knowledge supports going inward first, before you turn outwards to facilitate and manage your external knowledge. It may, therefore, be necessary to renegotiate the formal and psychological contract with yourself first, and then value your relationships with others carefully afterwards. In other words, know yourself first: know who you are, how you operate, your principles, your level of integrity and authenticity. The starting point would seem to be to value your inner knowledge first (as discussed in the first few chapters) before going on to build your network of relationships. Live your own integrity; understand your own values first; and then renegotiate your own contract with yourself before expanding outwards into your network and community. Neil Crofts (*www.authentictransformation. co.uk*) stresses the great importance of developing 'authentic leadership' in the modern business environment. He emphasises that to lead today you need complete personal integrity and confidence, based on deep self-knowledge. You also need to be fully digitally literate, and offer people inspiration and intrinsic motivation. Be the real you, and do not hide behind a mask even within the business environment. In this way you become authentic in your business dealings.

Valuing personal knowledge

You do not often hear people talking about valuing their own personal social capital derived from their own knowledge.

Why is it that the personal knowledge capital idea/concept is rarely openly discussed? Why are we leaving it to everyone else (individuals and organisations) to place value on the personal knowledge that we hold? To value your own personal knowledge (or current market value) requires that you map and identify your contacts and assess your own knowledge skills and expertise – as part of your outer personal knowledge. Personal capital is a label that also suggests that we are all responsible for our own choices! It is *your* choice to work for a particular company and accept a particular wage - it is an easy way to let the company tell you what you are worth (Cope 2000). Few people openly discuss valuing their own capital. It is important to be aware that a company can also devalue your personal capital. For instance, you apply for an international job in Asia and you are told on the phone that the salary is £55k (British pounds), and you accept the position. However, the next day the contract arrives via email offering £35k. You are astonished and write back asking if they have made an error. No, they say, you misheard them on the telephone. The phone line was crystal clear. Bargaining at this level of percentage is, of course, relatively unheard of in the West. To take the salary is to completely 'de-value' your own worth. Later you find the original advert posted on the web was the original £55k. Do not let others under-value you, if you think you are worth more. You make the decisions; they do not. Of course, there may have been a cultural dimension to this scenario, but the message is still the same. Do not let anyone else undermine your worth.

Awareness of your own personal core values is important, so that you remain true to yourself. This concept extends into your belief system, and may mean evaluating, judging and developing your own personal capital. Remember, what you want often changes at different stages of your career. Therefore, you need to be responsible for managing your own career, and regularly re-evaluate the knowledge and skills you have gained and your own current worth. If you have chosen a career path that motivates you, links to your talent, joy and happiness, then you have created the driver for personal and professional success. Being successful in the corporate world means taking personal control; choosing your own success criteria; creating a positive attitude and being aware that energy and enthusiasm lead to success.

Having a high level of intelligence but few contacts and behaving unethically will not get you far. Success usually equates to good ideas, energy and passion – people want to be around the infectiously lively people. Thus, being successful relates to enthusiasm. On the personal level, enthusiasm can be driven by 'living your joy', whether as a painter, writer, broadcaster, journalist, academic, or business executive. It is all personal to you: being the best at what you do comes from 'living your joy'. This is why you need to find out what will be 'your joy'. What is your own personal driver that leads you to be enthusiastic about what you do?

Reflective practice (business practice tools)

The best leaders and managers engage in the process of reflective practice. Reflective practice is a technique used in industry and taught in all business and management schools. Reflective practice enables the management practitioner to step back and reflect on decisions and behaviour taking place within a situation in the workplace. It differs from reflective individual thoughts because reflective practice means reflecting upon situations or external actions that have occurred in the workplace. Reflective practice enables you to take a moment, rewind the proceedings and analyse the situation, before taking the next step forward. Not only is this good for business managers and leaders, it is a requirement for personal development. Donald Schon (1983) suggested that the capacity to reflect on action so as to engage in a process of continuous learning was one of the defining characteristics of professional practice. He argued that the model of professional training that he termed 'technical rationality' – of charging students up with knowledge in training schools so that they could discharge it when they entered the world of practice – could perhaps be more aptly termed a battery model. Schon suggests that technical rationality has never been a particularly good description of how professionals think in action, and is quite inappropriate to practice in a fast-changing world. These 'indeterminate zones of practice' (Schon 1983) – uncertainty, uniqueness, value conflict – that cannot be navigated by technical rationality are central to professional practice because true competence in the swamp of uncertainty depends on learning from experience, and that entails reflection 'in action' (while doing something) and reflection 'on action' (after you have done it). Reflective practice leads to experiential learning which is about experiencing, reviewing and concluding on your current management practice by regularly reflecting on issues, dilemmas and practice. Take time out and step back to review and reflect on whether circumstances went well or not. In this way, you can constantly review situations by reflecting on either the positives or the negatives and deliberating on those you need to improve. Continuous improvement and learning from experience becomes part of your management practice. Reflective practice today may also mean reflecting upon proceedings taking place in both the physical and virtual space.

The knowledge worker can use the tools of reflective practice to regularly rewind the actions and scenarios which have taken place in the workplace. In this simple way, reflecting on practice helps to develop inner analytical reflective skills, which lead to experiential learning. It allows you to pause, stop and think, and act like a helicopter hovering overhead. This dynamic practice may lead to changing the direction in which you are proceeding. Reflection on practice is the stop button on the CD. Many times this practice can be helpful by simply using it as a pause mechanism in a business meeting. When asked to do something you are not sure about, simply say, 'I will reflect upon this'. This gives you time out and is good management practice. This time delay enables you to go away and think over the situation before agreeing, or gives you time to rethink and present the arguments that have influenced your decision to decline or accept the offer, before proceeding. Reflective practice is sound management practice that can lead you and your organisation in the right direction, simply by reviewing the proceedings to check whether or not you are on course, or need to change course. It may also form the basis of a lessons learnt knowledge repository in knowledge management, especially if the actions and reflections are recorded. Real knowledge is not merely facts or information but also includes a deep and rich mix of insights into a situation or practice.

Summary

The most important person is you! If you do not place value on yourself, who else will? As a professional in the workplace you need to value yourself before anyone else does. This means creating your boundaries. It means setting your own standards and levels of integrity; placing value on your own network; and valuing your own assets. In personal knowledge capital, valuing networking capabilities and raising conscious awareness of this has to be at the forefront of developing external knowledge. You can value the ties within your network of relationships and make serious decisions about which ties work for you. Taking time to consider your sphere of influence is also important in this process. Knowledge is acquired through the network of contacts acquired, but you need long-term sustainable relationships for overall success. Networking is a method of personal knowledge management. Most important of all is working with integrity, as you proceed. In addition, understanding and implementing reflective practice techniques in your business activities can lead to improvements in business practice as the cyclical approach to learning begins to emerge. Being aware of these business practices and embracing reflective management practices will ultimately help to make the good leader great.

Exercises for self-assessment

Self assess – by asking the following questions and carrying out the following tasks:

1. Can I place *market value* on my personal capital? Where do I position my personal capital in *the market*?
2. How do connections/network and relationships building work for you in your own organisation? What benefits do they bring? Give some examples.
3. What is meant by sphere of influence? Consider your own sphere of influence. How far does it stretch? Consider how far reaching or how limiting your network really is.
4. Draw a map with yourself in the middle and from it draw out your network and span of influence.

Can you think of your professional network in terms of strength of ties? Draw the links out on paper using different colour codes on the lines you draw, to emphasise the strength of each network tie. Make it like a spiral diagram. Look at it regularly and see who else you can add. As you do this, ask yourself the question: What is the strength of tie of this relationship?

5. In terms of your current working environment, where are you currently on the following scale? Self-assess yourself.

Hostile	Non-supportive	Neutral	Supportive	Very positive

6. Individual task – create a personal talent wheel

Map what you consider to be your personal knowledge and talent onto a wheel. The wheel may be in the form of a spider type diagram or a wheel shape, whichever you think is the most suitable to define your talents and skills.

(A future perspective)

Refine the diagram further and assess how this may further develop in the future?

7. What are your core values and beliefs? Write a list to remind yourself.

- Are you aware of your core beliefs and, if so, are you acting in accordance with your values?
- Do you think you are communicating these values to those around you in the workplace?
- Why are core values so important to culture in a workplace situation?
- Are you working in a culture that aligns to your values?

8. Think of an incident recently that did not go according to plan, then proceed to reflect on the situation. What went right according to plan? What could you have done differently? What changes and adjustments may you need to make because of your reflections? Are there lessons to be learnt? Use this reflective technique in the workplace on a regular basis to review the processes and steps you have taken.

7

Social capital and trust for a web environment

Abstract: The focus of this chapter is on social capital as part of third generation knowledge management. An understanding of what we mean by social capital within knowledge management, and an awareness of the value of relationships and issues of trust can change our view about what to value in the work environment. This chapter sets out to explain how to recognise social capital as you move into the virtual environment.

Key words: intellectual capital, social capital, relationships, trust.

We are moving into an era where valuing and identifying the intangible is becoming a priority in the work environment. Identifying the intangibles associated with this new era is imperative for the knowledge worker. In an era which embraces a blend of both the physical and virtual work activities, it is necessary to seize the opportunity to work with and exploit the intangibles in order to create value. Today, knowledge management includes intellectual capital under its umbrella, and because of this a new vocabulary has emerged where we talk about labels such as human and social capital. At the forefront of The outer path of personal knowledge capital is the need to identify the source of intangibles, particularly when using the web environment.

Intellectual capital

Intellectual capital is a label used to identify the intangible assets within an organisation and to break them down into meaningful sections. Exploring this concept enables us to understand how it currently relates to knowledge management and knowledge creation. Stewart (1998), Sveiby (1997) and Edvinsson (1997, cited in McElroy 2003) are representative of the early writers in the intellectual capital movement. Edvinsson (1997) emphasises that intellectual capital includes all the processes and the assets which are not normally shown on the balance sheet, including the intangible assets in modern accounting (mainly trademarks, patents and brands). As a main theorist in the area of intellectual capital, Stewart (1998), an American writer, has been a pioneer in the field, exploring how to manage, reveal and unlock the value of hidden assets. He considers intellectual capital to be intellectual material in terms of the knowledge, information, intellectual property and experience that can be put to use to create wealth. Stewart, like Saint-Onge (1996), divides intellectual capital into three broad categories: human capital, structural capital and customer capital. However, Stewart prefers to make an operational distinction between human capital and customer capital, suggesting that customer capital is the value of an organisation's relationship with the people with whom it does business and this includes valuing relationships with suppliers as well as brand equity. However, little discussion emerges as to how this packaged human capital will be developed, or how intellectual capital may be facilitated by the new tools and technologies. The advances made by Edvinsson and Stewart do not take into account another major component of intangible value now commonly recognised as social capital.

Social capital

Social capital is part of the umbrella of intellectual capital, and may mean placing value on the social interactions. This is why very often individuals who are the most difficult to replace in the company, and who hold high value, are those who have created high levels of social capital through the communities and groups in which they interact. The value comes from their ability to network effectively and participate within groups so that they are in effect recognised for their contribution through the mobilisation of their social assets. Social capital refers to the collective abilities derived from social networks (Huysman and Wulf 2006). Nahapiet and Ghoshal (1998) suggest that a specific definition of the term is hard to come by, but the definition Nahapiet and Ghoshal relate to is that social capital means the actual and potential resources embedded within, available through, and derived from networks of relationships possessed by an individual or social unit, and they view social capital as a relational resource. Therefore, Nahapiet and Ghoshal's definition of social capital comprises both the network and the assets that may be mobilised through that network. This is equivalent to an organisational member who has created a strongly established network of industry leaders to call upon. Different attributes arise within three clusters – the structural, relational and cognitive dimensions of social capital (Nahapiet and Ghoshal 1998). The above writers suggest that social capital is a relational resource and as such its development is affected by how factors such as time, interaction and interdependence shape the evolution of social relationships. McElroy (2003) discusses social capital theory and emphasises that there are two major schools of thought, namely the *egocentric* and the *socio-centric perspective*, and he suggests that the egocentric perspective is a useful view to attach to social capital creation occurring within an online environment. McElroy suggests that, unlike other forms of intellectual capital, social capital points to the *value of relationships* between people in firms, and between firms and other firms inclusive of *trust, reciprocity, shared values, networking and norms*. These are all things that add value and develop knowledge. McElroy uses the label *social innovation capital* to refer to the structural manner in which whole social systems (firms) organise themselves around – and carry out – the production and integration of new knowledge. Value creation is therefore social in nature and is embedded in social relations and the way people and systems organise themselves despite some varying interpretations of the definition. This type of value added can, therefore, be exploited in contemporary organisations by using these processes as strategies, in order to encourage greater levels of competitive advantage. Awareness of social capital as an organisational asset that is social in nature is important, as this enables us to fully exploit it. Ultimately this is crucial for the knowledge worker within the current technological learning environment where the potential already exists to exploit relationships, at the heart of which are issues of trust and shared values. Awareness of social capital may lead to exploiting a type of innovation capital within the environment as part of external personal knowledge capital.

It is essential to understand and be aware of value, in the form of social capital, in what very often turns out to be the communities and networks in which you operate. Interestingly, when Stewart discusses human capital he suggests that communities of practice can also be viewed as part of human capital development. However, Huysman and Wulf (2006) believe that it is important to differentiate between human capital and social capital, and suggest that human capital refers to individual ability, while social capital refers to *collective ability* derived from social networks. This interpretation suggests that the individual knowledge workers can be viewed in terms of their human capital contribution, while their network of meaningful contacts supports social capital. Social capital in relation to knowledge sharing shifts attention from individuals sharing knowledge to communities as knowledge-sharing entities, where community and social networks are seen as the prime source of a sense of membership and commitment (Wenger 1998, cited in Huysman and Wulf 2006). It is, therefore, possible to create and manage communities in order to generate new knowledge, and innovative ideas. It may be that within the confines of a community, members interact with one another to create new knowledge. The link between the two concepts of social capital and community needs to be emphasised. In particular the question which arises is: how does social capital develop in the virtual environment?

Social capital and the virtual environment

Web environments and web tools have now developed to facilitate social aspects of networking including tools for online forums and space for instant chat. Therefore, it is important to become aware of how best to make use of these facilitates for what we now call third generation knowledge management. Indeed, this is supported by all forms of mobile technology. Designing for managed social capital innovation facilitated by the web technologies and tools is a major step forward in terms of innovative ways of learning in the contemporary organisation.

Identifying social and human capital as part of Knowledge Creation Assets may be a key element for knowledge workers in the future, as greater use is made of information and communication technology (ICT) to support learning. Limited discussion has emerged on the development of social capital development in terms of ICT and the web environment. Identifying social and intellectual capital and Knowledge Creation Assets through the use of the web tools and technologies may lead to greater understanding of the learning processes taking place in a contemporary organisation, particularly at the micro-operational level. Thus, in relation to the web platform, and the tools and software available within this area, exploring the relationship between the web environment and the generation of social and intellectual capital is vital. In particular, we need to understand how to maximise human and social capital by using the web environment available. Kok (2007) believes that bringing intellectual capital, knowledge management and enabling technologies together is an exciting challenge for leaders wishing to create an information age institution. Appreciating social capital concepts and how they can be developed online supports an understanding of the potential for intangible value in a twenty-first-century organisation.

Relationships and trust

If we are valuing relationships in either networks or communities (including virtual communities) we need to understand what makes a relationship work. All relationships are managed due to the level of trust encountered. Relationships occur at a personal level in terms of the friendships that we all encounter and develop, and also at an individual and group professional level in our working relationships with colleagues.

Underpinning any discussion on relationships within the social capital umbrella is the need to consider what makes a relationship work. Nahapiet and Ghoshal (1998), McElroy (2003), Lang (2004) and Huysman and Wulf (2006) all discuss issues of trust, trustworthiness or interpersonal trust underpinning social capital. Valuing relationships within networks, communities and organisational culture is a crucial element for social capital. The concept of trust is a main tenet for relationships in organisations which enables effective communication and knowledge sharing. Abrams et al. (2003) highlight that interpersonal trust can be defined as the *'willingness of a party to be vulnerable'*. Two dimensions of trust that promote knowledge creation and sharing are *benevolence* (you care about me and take an interest in my well-being and goals) and *competence* where you have relevant expertise and can be depended upon to know what you are talking about (Abrams et al. 2003). According to Abrams et al. *'benevolence-based trust'* allows one to query a colleague in depth without fear of damage to self-esteem or reputation. In addition, he argues that people must also trust that the persons they turn to have sufficient expertise to offer solutions. *'Competence-based trust'* allows one to feel confident that the person sought out knows what he/she is talking about and is worth listening to and learning from (Abrams et al. 2003). An important issue arising is: How do we facilitate the intangible assets such as trust within relationships? The answer lies in first being aware of the significance of these relationships. The environment created between individuals should be highly conducive to creating trusting relationships at the micro level. Relationships and trust created within the environment may be at the heart of the learning community and culture, but at the same time form part of social and intellectual capital creation. Creating a benevolent (or caring) environment may therefore be a contributing factor to developing trusting relationships within an organisational context. The competitive environment may at the organisation level be a stifling environment for community spirit, good relations, or trust developing between colleagues, and thus impede knowledge sharing within the organisation. On the other hand, the collegiate organisation may embrace community spirit and long-term trusting relationships, which facilitate knowledge sharing. Renewed awareness of the value of trust and social interactions and how these elements may be maximised enables the professional knowledge worker to create more value, and work more effectively. The question is: How are we able to value, manage and design for social capital, which develops within the interactive dynamic virtual space?

Trust, conversation and learning in the online environment

Designing tools to support knowledge sharing should take into serious consideration the potential motivational barriers to sharing knowledge which may exist in the organisation due to status differences, lack of trust, or lack of perceived reciprocity and lack of respect. Lang (2004) argues that arms' length relationships are suitable for the transfer of codified knowledge where uncertainty is low, whereas social contexts can be those where interpersonal ties are highly embedded. When designing a knowledge-based environment, social capital creation may be a process that in particular derives from the relationships and interactions built on the issue of trust within the interactive space created within the web environment. Trust underpins all human relationships, it impinges on professional networking and it underpins collaboration in professional communities. In this way, trust relies on integrity, reliability and consistency not only in personal but in professional life. If you do not build trust, do not expect to go far in your professional life, as a lack of trust may backfire.

Effectively using interactive tools to generate knowledge creation in the interactive online environment may relate to the value derived from social and intellectual capital. This is what McElroy (2003) calls third generation knowledge management and it arises from exploiting the latest web tools for synchronous (instant messaging) and asynchronous (threaded discussion) purposes in order to generate conversation, reflection and new ideas for innovation. Social capital arises online as members share their mental models, reflect, and gain ideas and insight generated from the conversation, in order to reinforce those ideas. These features would support what Von Krogh et al. (2000) call conversation and dialogue at the heart of knowledge creation processes, and what Laurillard (2007) calls a conversational framework at the heart of learning. The conversational framework is a concept which very much relates to a learning environment and, in particular, to learning pedagogy which is contemporary and interactive in style rather than didactive (meaning spoon-fed approaches). In this way, it is possible to see the development of third generation knowledge management in the learning environment with an emphasis on valuing conversation and dialogue. The exploitation of conversation in the interactive space within the virtual environment is a key component of human and social capital development as part of intellectual capital theory.

Summary

Identifying and placing value on intangible assets is a key component within knowledge creation theory, knowledge management and personal knowledge management.

Intellectual capital is a broad concept, encompassing a variety of interpretations and sub-labels within this particular genre. The renewed awareness of the value of social capital and how it may be exploited enables organisational members to create more value. The emphasis on social capital generation highlights the need to create good relationships that are underpinned by trust and integrity. Design for managed social capital innovation facilitated by the web technologies and tools is a major step forward in terms of innovative ways of learning in a twenty-first-century organisation.

Exercises

1. How far do you currently value the relationships you have developed with colleagues in terms of social capital generation?

2. How far does trust extend in terms of your relationship with your current colleagues in the work environment, and in your personal life? Which colleagues do you trust the most, and in what way? Make a list.

3. Does the environment you work in cultivate a knowledge sharing culture? In what way does this occur? Why is this important?

4. Can you encourage the organisation/department to share? What sort of barriers are in existence?

5. If you cannot entice the organisation to share, do you want to work in a non-sharing culture where there is a lack of trust?

The magic box

Abstract: In a world where new ideas and solutions are a way to create new business and solve problems the magic box is key. This is a metaphor that can be used visually to bring to mind a set of processes that could encourage creative solutions. By visualising the metaphor an array of processes and ideas may come to mind.

Key words: magic box, ideas, innovation, social interaction.

What we all need is a magic box! Look inside the box - and it begins to solve your problems – because it is a magic box! Inside are bright ideas, insight, solutions and knowledge. This box is magical because it enables you to think of ways to find creative and innovative solutions to problems and issues. The magic box acts as a visual metaphor as part of tacit knowledge as discussed by Nonaka and colleagues, and, as such, one can generate new ideas and solutions. The magic box forms part of the Knowledge Cube in the later chapters. This chapter establishes the magic box as a visual metaphor for innovative solutions in a business environment.

Ideas

The new currency for twenty-first-century management includes 'ideas and insight' – the 'intangibles', for the new

91

The magic box

The Magic Box

Figure 8.1   The magic box

economy. Innovative ideas keep businesses alive. Amidon (2003) suggests that an innovation culture is one where ideas are the new currency, indicating that ideas can generate new value creation and wealth. It is ideas that make a good company great. Amidon does not, however, mention concepts in terms of social capital or give specific details as to how the 'ideas' currency will be achieved in practice. Dvir and Pashner (2004) suggest that innovation is the process of turning knowledge and ideas into value. Ideas are an integral aspect of the human experience, a concentration of concepts and intuitions, and good ideas can generate new value creation and wealth (Davis cited in Amidon, 2003). Because of this, employees should be looking for dynamic individuals who can help push the business forward in new ways. Davis (2003) argues that within a de facto market place, ideas within the enterprise can circulate freely or they can be encumbered. Choo and Bontis (2002) emphasise the relationship between innovation and knowledge creation, stating that innovation consists of new ideas that have been

transformed or implemented as products, processes or services generating value for the firm, and that ideas are formed through a deep interaction among people in environments that have the conditions to enable knowledge creation. This implies that there is a clear link between innovation and the environment and the conditions created to support these processes. If we relate these concepts to the use of web technologies, a whole new currency may develop, guided by knowledge workers themselves. Using and visualising the magic box reminds us to think of creative solutions arising through new ideas which are formed through using conversation, possibly in communities. Visualising the magic box reminds us that rich ideas are the foundation for success in the knowledge economy. The visualisation process itself is, of course, a type of emotional tacit knowledge. Ideas arrive while conversing, and this is the subject of the next section.

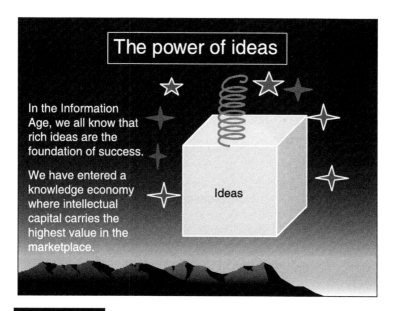

| **Figure 8.2** | The power of ideas |

Conversation

How do we facilitate these ideas? Without the opportunity to converse there is a lack of communication within business environments, which leads to a lack of energy as the organisation becomes static rather than dynamic. At the heart of the conversational process is the prospect of 'tuning' in to new ideas for creativity and innovation. Underpinning conversation and dialogue is the prospect of sharing your ideas with others, while gleaning new ideas to improve the business. Conversation is at the heart of tacit-to-tacit knowledge in the socialisation process, and is one way of sharing and distributing knowledge. Von Krogh et al. (2000) highlight the importance of conversation as an enabler for knowledge creation. If conversation and dialogue support reflecting and modifying insights, rethinking mental models and sharing new ideas, then conversation has to be at the heart of learning and knowledge creation because it generates valuable assets. Dialogue involves individual knowledge

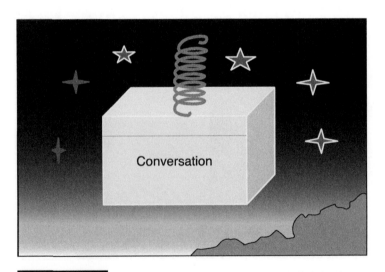

Figure 8.3   The box of ideas

workers conversing within either physical or online space, while sharing their views and mental models on a particular topic. As the two parties share their views in this manner, eventually one party may decide, upon reflection, to modify their outlook. It is not important whether this occurs in the physical or the virtual environment – what is important is that communication through conversation does takes place, so that the process of sharing ideas to gain insight begins to ignite.

With the development of the interactive web technologies we are able to expand and exchange ideas through managed conversation which results in a type of intangible currency. This takes place within a community built on relationships developed within the virtual ecology. In this respect, the interactive web environment may support dialogue by using web features such as the blog, live chat or threaded discussion. Skryme (1999) proposes that it is a content space (relationships and repositories), and suggests that web conferencing tools and knowledge management suites are helping this integration.

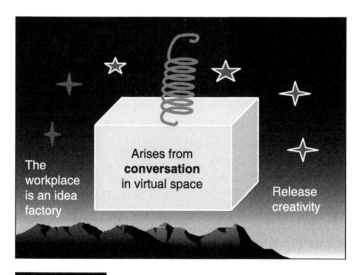

Figure 8.4 The box of ideas in virtual space

Sharing ideas may lead to modifying mental models established in our heads, and adapting these mental footprints may lead to new ideas and learning. Dialogue is such an easy way to share knowledge, especially as we converse and discuss ideas with colleagues and friends all day long in the work environment. Raising your level of awareness to the potential of conversation as a means to share tacit knowledge helps you – the knowledge worker – to be more sensitive to using this mechanism for knowledge sharing. Eventually this may stimulate new ways of thinking about a topic, and result in new learning and a modification of views. In this way, new insights and ideas are generated, as the process occurs on a one-to-one, one-to-many, or many-to-many basis. In this process the magic box mechanism (visual metaphor) can be quickly utilised. Conversation can and should be valued, and ultimately can be managed for knowledge sharing in the business environment. Conversation is important in a business context; however, as on the world stage, the only channel of communication is diplomatic. Diplomatic conversation leads to new views and solutions to solve old problems. As a result healing takes place, and you transfer problems into learning experiences. It is the emphasis on conversation for both learning and knowledge creation that is crucial. If a key element of learning and knowledge sharing is the emphasis on conversation and dialogue, then this element is crucial for the knowledge worker in the business context. The magic box visual metaphor reminds us to consider these tools for creative solutions.

Knowledge, blogs and social interaction

Today, young professionals are using (or are aware of) the interactive media, in the form of Web 2.0 and 3.0 which comprises social media including blogs, wikis, Facebook, Flickr and Linkedin (to mention a few), while at the same time using mobile technologies to communicate. The assumption in third generation knowledge management is that learning is fundamentally the result of our social interactions (Garcia 2009). The assumption in emerging models is that learning – perceived as knowledge creation – is collective, constructive and conversational (Scott 2005, cited in Garcia 2009). Negotiation and the social skills (such as communication, networking and collaboration skills) attached to it are part of the new reality of e-learning environments and internet interactions happening worldwide on a 24/7 basis – an increasing flow of continuous and creative interaction (Garcia 2009). Garcia suggests that computer-networked workplaces are increasingly embracing a number of versatile generic tools which are also used for educational communication such as blogging, Q&A postings, email, skype calls, chat rooms and radio chat broadcastings, discussion boards, wiki-based platforms within virtual communities, webinars and other similar technologies. These learning tools bring new levels and modes of understanding through virtual interactions. What is clear is that these tools and technologies form part of the knowledge workers personal ecology, and thereby support knowledge creation and learning.

Blogs have currently become synonymous with personal knowledge management. Why not use the latest tools and technologies to encourage reflective thought, dialogue and conversation? The arrival of online tools for creating blogs and web journals enables their users to reflect and record their thoughts instantly. Blogs are a means of recording your own reflective thoughts and posting them on the web. As an individual tool for personal knowledge capital, blogs are immensely useful. This may link to a time-line in terms of thinking and reflective practice. Reflective practice is an important management development tool, and forms part of knowledge management practice in lessons learnt. Blogs may raise levels of self-awareness, so why not make use of the new tools out there? In this way the new technologies are providing opportunities for sharing, reflecting, distributing and storing information and knowledge. This capacity may lead to new ways of operating and greater levels of innovation and effectiveness for the individual professional to exploit. An opportunity not to be missed!

Postings appear all over the world from individual knowledge workers, business professionals, pop stars, journalists and reporters covering daily and hourly events. Blogging is primarily known as an instrument for personal publishing, reaching a broad and often unknown audience without pushing content on them (Efimova 2010). What is crucial about the blog is its distributive nature which enables the user to share thoughts with a wider audience. Thus the blog tool is a knowledge-sharing device: using personal knowledge management technology tools may help members of the organisation to be more self-sufficient. Efimova (2010) states that weblogs are often discussed as a tool that supports bottom-up knowledge management, and discusses how they might be useful to tap into insights that escape more formal documents, to see faces behind ideas, to have conversations across hierarchical boundaries and to connect with experts found in unexpected parts of an organisation or outside it. Although blogging is personal, most of its advantages are the result of being part of an ecosystem, where weblogs are connected not only by links, but also by relations between bloggers (Efimova 2010). Efimova discusses blogs in terms of a space to incubate ideas, and capture those ideas into a trusted repository, providing sense-making capabilities, getting things done; visible expertise and practical help. Further, Efimova suggests that these relations do not appear

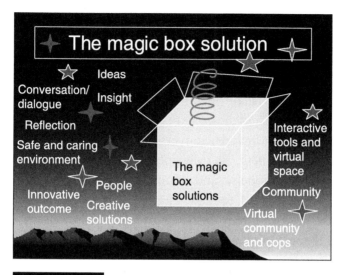

Figure 8.5   The magic box solution

automatically: it takes time and effort before one can enjoy the social effects of blogging. It is, therefore, important to find ways and means to blog effectively. New practice should encourage the development of one's own smart working practices.

It is up to you to create your own environment for your own personal knowledge capital system. Being aware of the importance of the intangible assets you have, and how to manage them, puts you in a better position. You can value the tools, including mobile tools, where this social interaction may develop. Being aware of these issues changes the way you do things, and how you react. Managing your own ecology eventually puts you in a position of control. In other words, you can take control of your own destiny – now you know how to assess what is valuable for you. This is external personal knowledge management, part of knowledge capital, and includes inner and outer knowledge.

Summary

Ideas as currency form part of social capital generation, and lead to knowledge and innovation. The magic box is a symbol and visual metaphor for thinking managed conversation. Inside the box are creative solutions. The tools to achieve this include conversation in the physical and virtual environment. Sharing ideas leads to modifying our own mental models, and modification of these mental footprints can lead to new ideas and learning. Although various positions may be held strongly, solutions can be found through dialogue. Without dialogue and conversation there is no magic bullet.

Exercises

Ask yourself the following questions:

1. Do you currently value conversation and dialogue in the workplace as a way of generating new ideas?
2. How far do you value the relationships you have developed with colleagues?
3. The magic box is a visual process – can you explain this in terms of knowledge creation?
4. What social network tools might you use to manage your own personal ecology, and why?

9

Community and culture

Abstract: Today there are a whole array of different types of communities emerging in organisations. What types of community do you want to be involved in? What type of design issues are involved due to using these communities? This chapter discusses some of these issues before looking at the importance of culture for knowledge-sharing purposes.

Key words: types of community, communities of practice, culture.

We have talked about the importance of conversation in business. Conversation occurs in groups and meetings in a business environment, and today it also takes place in communities. Thus social capital in the form of social interactions may arise in a variety of physical and virtual communities. Communities offer a powerful mechanism for sharing and collaboration and may hold a place in the structure of the organisation formally or informally. Communities are a mechanism to help change occur in the physical or virtual environment.

Community, trust and social capital

Knowledge and insight arises in communities, as it is here that actors on the stage interact with one another through dialogue and conversation, forming relationships that are the cornerstone of knowledge creation. Communities develop over time based on the relationships and interactions that are formed and shaped among the members. Knowledge flows and is transferred in and between the community members. Physical and virtual communities generate social interactions to create the intangible value that we are now looking for in the business environment. Communities of practice form part of human capital within intellectual capital theory (Stewart 1998) and, because of this, Stewart argues that the relationship between individual learning and an organisation's human capital, not just its stock of knowledge, but its capacity to innovate, involves groups even more than individuals. In this way, the corporate assets are social in origin, and innovative outcomes are linked to particular groups, rather than just to individuals. There is a link between groups of knowledge workers within a vibrant community, developing good relationships, socialising and generating social capital, and the value added this creates for corporate organisations. Social capital in relation to knowledge sharing shifts its attention from individuals sharing knowledge to communities as knowledge-sharing entities, where community and social networks are seen as the prime source of a sense of membership and commitment (Wenger 1998, cited in Huysman and Wulf 2006). It is therefore desirable to create and facilitate communities in order to generate new knowledge, and incubate new and innovative ideas.

Added to this, social capital elements arising from relationships are clearly linked to the interactive dynamic spaces on the web and are supported by strength of ties and relationships formed in the online community. *Weak social ties* in the community and virtual learning environment lead to less social coherence so that less social capital emerges, while *strong social ties* and trust within the community lead to higher levels of social capital. However, this depends on the type of community you want to create in the first place. The quality of the community is, of course, fed by the quality of the online leadership. The importance of leadership and the skills and characteristics necessary are fully discussed in Chapter 11 (Table 11.1). It is proposed that when creating an online web environment, apart from taking into consideration the vital role played by the virtual leader, one of the main goals should be to exploit a design for social capital creation through the collaborative interactive features within the online system. The question is: How are we able to value, manage and design for social capital, which develops within the interactive dynamic virtual online forums and communities where conversation flows? The answer is that first we need to be aware of the value of social capital, and second, we need to decide what sort of community is appropriate for the business model or business context we wish to be developed.

Types of web-based community

The idea of virtual communities has arisen in the past decade because of the development of new tools and features, such as threaded discussion and live chat, within the new technologies. The question is: Can community aspects facilitate knowledge sharing and knowledge creation online? These tools enable interactions to occur, including insight to gain new ideas that will impact on cultural change. Within this space ideas and reflective thoughts can be bounced around in order to support the emergence of new views. With the arrival of interactive dynamic online communication tools, community aspects have become a key consideration for the design of a knowledge-focused web environment. It is the community members themselves who interact to share knowledge, insight and ideas, while at the same time the community leader or champion facilitates, sustains, and helps to create a knowledge flow and synergy within the community. Various types of community arise including communities of practice; e-learning communities; wisdom communities; micro communities; knowledge communities and network communities (see Table 9.1).

Communities of practice

In today's organisation it is important to be aware of what constitutes value added in terms of sharing common practice between members of the organisation. Those members who have a keen interest in one specialised area may want to share their practice with like-minded members. In doing so, they may wish to use a community mechanism, either virtual or physical, to share practice. An example of a community of practice is a group of members who meet regularly to discuss a common passion, and as such facilitate learning or discuss problems associated with a specific issue. The community may emerge bottom-up through self-organisation or top-down organised by management. Communities may vary in size and may emerge formally or informally. The community may meet informally over coffee in the cafeteria, or they may take a more formal approach creating time for business meetings. Creating a community of practice in an organisation provides a mechanism for members to meet and share common practice. Within the community of practice there are elements of 'acceptance' of new members by the community so that acceptance into the community means acknowledgement of a member's area of expertise. Acceptance plays a key part in communities of practice, where the practice (passion, interest, expertise) of those entering into this domain is validated by the other members. For example, these interests at the heart of the community could be focused upon e-learning, mechanical engineering, quality standards or technical design. Acceptance into the community may ultimately be a restriction, as there are elements of exclusivity arising. Communities of practice, however, to their advantage may span across the organisation hierarchy and may easily by-span the formal span of control within the organisation. This makes them a powerful mechanism for organisational change. However, it is the power of this type of special interest group to make things happen that makes them a force to be reckoned with. Wenger (2000) acknowledges that the purpose of the community of practice is to create a cycle of application, assessment, reflection and renewal by which an organisation learns through action to identify and take responsibility for key areas of knowledge. This implies that communities of practice play a key role in the learning process occurring within the organisation, by providing a framework by which individuals collaborate and collectively focus on areas of expertise. Corporate assets can be social in origin and communities of practice enable these assets to be developed in order to facilitate the learning process and support knowledge creation. These social interactions form part of social and intellectual capital.

With regard to design principles for communities, Wenger et al. (2002) discuss various principles including: the aliveness of the community; evolutionary design; distributed leadership; participation across multiple structures; formal and informal; design for value; a participative emergent approach; building on existing culture; cultivating informal structures; and knowledge which is social, individual and dynamic. Thus Wenger et al. (2002) focus on community enabling and an overview of factors that relate to the design of a web environment ranging from aliveness to culture itself.

What makes for the rejection of the communities of practice theory in educational practice is that in terms of the design of a knowledge web environment it takes time for the community members to get to know one another. This time aspect is not necessarily practical because in education students attend lectures on modules usually delivered within a relatively short time frame. With regard to knowledge creation theory, Von Krogh et al. (2000) also discuss a 'micro-community' developing within small groups to enable knowledge creation. Within the micro-community, knowledge can be created in collective communities through processes of guided thinking via dialogue, reflection and insight to gain new ideas, to impact on cultural change. However, this concept of community is soon rejected as a design principle because the size of the community group is limited to five to seven people. Community membership is usually much larger than the small size specified. Apart from the focus on communities of practice and micro communities, some writers also discuss the concept of e-learning, wisdom, knowledge and network communities.

The e-learning community

Web technology tools have now developed to facilitate social aspects of networking such as online forums and space for online chat. These tools support online interactions in the form of dialogue and conversation to take shape within the e-learning environment. Mynatt, Adler, Ito and O'Day (1997) in their discussion on network communities advocate design dimensions that require a balance between technological and social elements, where network communities emerge from the intertwining of sociality and technology in ways that make it difficult to separate these individual influences clearly. Hardaker and Smith (2002) stress that building e-learning communities is viewed as the fundamental driver of both explicit and tacit knowledge creation and that this reflects the rich forms of technology now being released into the mass market through the internet. E-learning is seen as a driver of knowledge creation across unstructured virtual communities (Hardaker and Smith 2002). These e-learning communities should be taken into consideration for the knowledge-focused web environment and are a response to demand at an operational level. E-learning communities support problem-based learning in online education.

The wisdom community

The concept of a knowledge community suggests a community of intelligence or wisdom emerging. Gunawardena et al. (2006) introduce the concept of a wisdom community, based on work carried out on a graduate course. They discuss the development of a new instructional design model called Wiscom. The Wiscom model is community centred, which suggests that community-centred environments offer a new perspective to create a supportive context within which learners can navigate the process of learning by collaborating and becoming collectively wise. The Wiscom model is supported by socio-constructivist learning theories, and combines the cognitive, affective and social dimensions of learning to create an environment that fosters reflection, sharing, dialogue, mutual trust, respect, commitment and common goals for knowledge innovation and transformational learning (Gunawardena et al. 2006). These authors claim that Wiscom encourages learners to become reflective thinkers engaged in the active construction of knowledge. However, they do not explain in detail the size of the community, or boundaries within the community, membership issues, or how to become reflective thinkers engaged in the active construction of knowledge.

However, a wisdom community may be taken into consideration for the design of a knowledge web environment depending on the flexibility required.

The knowledge community

McDermott (1999b), a North American writer, introduces the knowledge community and argues that to leverage knowledge we need to focus on the community that owns it, and the people who use it, rather than the knowledge itself. Therefore, ownership and human elements are crucial. McDermott (1999b) argues that learning from past experience, sharing insights, or even sharing 'best practice' is always rooted in the present, representing 'the thinking we are doing now'. Moreover, he suggests that insights from the past have always mediated the present living act 'of knowing'. McDermott suggests that value added resides within the community among the members of the community as they form relationships and share tacit-to-tacit knowledge via conversation, sharing ideas, insight and reflection. McDermott (1999a) suggests that to solve problems, professionals piece information together and reflect on their experiences, generate insights and use those insights to resolve them. The moderator's role in communities is very often to facilitate conversation, encourage reflective thinking and change individual and group mental models in order to allow new ways of thinking about the world to emerge.

McDermott also highlights the impact of a knowledge community on an organisation, suggesting that the spread of cultural change may lead to major new developments for the organisation. This implies that communities have a major part to play in changing and developing organisations, and awareness of the mechanisms of change is important to the contemporary organisation. McDermott does not stress a minimum or maximum size for the community and this shows some flexibility, nor does he discuss acceptance in the community as a criterion for membership, as does Wenger. Therefore, a knowledge community could be considered as a useful concept in design terms for developing a web environment.

The network community

Another type of community to add to the debate is the network community. Mynatt et al. (1997) suggest that network communities embody a particular design direction in supporting collaborative activity. Mynatt and colleagues introduce three issues. First, network communities require some sort of articulation of a persistent sense of location which is resolved through spatial metaphors. In terms of managing spatial relations, people inhabit both the online space and the real world simultaneously (Mynatt et al. 1997). When designing there should be coherence between real and virtual worlds as well as taking into consideration the challenges of migrating social practices from real to virtual worlds. Mynatt et al. (1997) stress that network communities are conglomerates of people and practices – neither transparently virtual nor physical, but rather a myriad of technical and social structures and conventions. Second, Mynatt et al. (1997) suggest that as users inhabit both real and virtual spaces, network communities require a complicated management of markers to link elements (i. e. people, environment, objects and actions). Third, there is the problem of community and social cohesion, with a need for flexible couplings between technical mechanisms and social acts that can evolve over time. The first and second issues of spatial metaphors, and the user inhabitation of real and virtual space, are met by the concept of 'Ba' (Nonaka, Toyama and Konno (2000) and Von Krogh et al. (2000)). Earlier it was proposed that the Ba metaphor be used to identify the creation of mental, virtual and physical space within current practice as a design element, and this fits with Mynatt's first and second issues. However, within Mynatt's theory there is no discussion on the limitation of the size of the community, flexibility within it, or membership acceptance as prerequisites to entry. The design elements discussed encourage the use of community aspects within the spatial elements for both real and virtual space. Therefore, Mynatt and colleagues' (1997) concept of a network community fits well within a design that emphasises the unifying aspects of physical and virtual space. It is suggested that knowledge communities, wisdom communities and various network communities have open membership to give more flexibility and this makes them more attractive. However, communities of practice and micro-communities may not be suitable when proposing communities in terms of design principles, as they have restrictions due to membership acceptance and small numbers.

Table 9.1   Types of community

Type	Author and date	Emphasis
E-Learning communities	(Hardaker and Smith (2002); Hardaker and Smith (2001)	Hardaker and Smith (2001) propose that to sustain knowledge management across organisations that are distributive in structure, e-learning communities provide the fundamental drivers. In other words, e-learning communities are a mechanism for knowledge creation. This e-learning community aspect can be established in the threaded discussion space where members reside, interact and form relationships within the community.

Type	Author and date	Emphasis
Wisdom communities	Gunawardena et al. (2006)	Gunawardena and colleagues encourage learning to foster reflective thinking, sharing, dialogue, trust, respect and commitment for innovate and transformative learning to engage in active construction of knowledge. However, Gunawardena et al. (2006) do not explain in detail the size of the community, membership issues, or boundaries within the community, which is very limiting.
Communities of practice	Wenger et al. (2002)	In terms of design principles for communities, Wenger et al. (2002) discuss principles which include the following: 'aliveness' of the community; evolutionary design principles; distributed leadership; participation across multiple structures; the dance of formal and informal; design for value; a participative emergent approach; building on existing culture; cultivating informal structures; knowledge which is social as well as individual; and knowledge which is dynamic. 'Aliveness' results from choreographing the dance between the informal professional passions and aspirations of practitioners, and the organisation's formal operational requirements, as well as between feelings of 'identity and belonging' at the community level and 'goals and objectives' at the organisational level (Wenger et al. 2002). Design limitations due to issues of acceptance by membership.
Micro-community	Von Krogh et al. (2000)	Highlight a 'micro-community' developing within small groups to enable knowledge creation. Limited by size – five to six members – not always suitable.

(Continued)

Table 9.1		Types of community *(Continued)*
Type	**Author and date**	**Emphasis**
Knowledge community	McDermott (1999a)	'Value added' resides within the community among the members as they form relationships and share tacit-to-tacit knowledge through conversation and dialogue, sharing ideas, insight and reflection. No restrictions occur regarding issues of acceptance or membership in the community.
Network communities	Mynatt et al. (1997)	The goal here is to consider network communities as one type of emergent and viable design direction in supporting community. They suggest that as users inhabit both real and virtual spaces, network communities require a complicated management of markers that link elements (people, environment, objects and actions). There is a problem of community and social cohesion and they stress the need for flexible couplings between technical mechanisms and social acts that can evolve over time.

Culture

When you take up a new job role, you may wish to carefully consider whether you will be working in a supportive cultural environment. Why is culture so important? Because if you accept a new job where you cannot grow, learn, create, collaborate and innovate or dare to make a mistake in a non-supportive environment, it is doubtful if you will be happy. We are talking about being able to share knowledge and collaborating here so you can feel comfortable and supported.

It is hard to share ideas if you feel that you are not appreciated by those around you. Therefore, before you take up a new post, it is wise to do your homework and make as much effort as possible to find out about the culture in which you may find yourself. Working in an amenable caring culture will in the long run provide a better work–life balance in terms of 'mind and body'. This mind versus body thinking is part of knowledge management and becomes relevant when we focus on personal knowledge creation.

In knowledge management terms, culture is key to sharing knowledge. However, it is the inbuilt assumptions and invisible core values of the culture that impinge on the individual's manner of behaving within the organisation. Any culture is based on a set of assumptions and beliefs about how the world works, and Schein (1985, 1992) defines five categories: (1) the nature of the environment; (2) the nature of reality or truth; (3) time and space; (4) human activity and (5) human nature. Schein (1985, 1992) summarises a formal definition for culture as a pattern of shared basic assumptions invented, discovered or developed by a given group as it learns to cope with problems of external adaptation and internal integration. These assumptions are, therefore, transferred and taught to new members of the group as the correct way to perceive, think and feel in relation to various problems. A good example of this would be an organisation I used to visit on a regular basis. It had a young workforce who were enthusiastic and fired up, but the culture was very conformist to say the least. It was so conformist as to be almost verging on a type of corporate communism. In an environment such as this it is hard to challenge the norm, and that means new and creative ideas may be stifled. It was a culture of conformity despite the rhetoric. A lot depends upon culture. Shared values are at the heart of collaborative working and knowledge sharing. It is important, therefore, to assess the culture to see if you are aligned to it. Allee (1997) believes a culture of learning and knowledge sharing does not happen by accident, suggesting that the *old practices* of hoarding knowledge are so *deeply ingrained* in business that changing the culture is a major component of shifting into a learning mind set. What is important in a knowledge culture is a climate of trust and openness in an environment where learning and experimentation are valued (Allee 1997). Reviewing an organisational culture is, therefore, important in terms of understanding an organisation's knowledge sharing capacity.

Assessing organisational cultural readiness for knowledge sharing

Although assessing a culture needs to take place from a personal perspective it is also important from a managing, implementing and sharing knowledge perspective. Assessing the organisation's cultural readiness is an important factor when planning to implement a knowledge management initiative. Therefore, an organisation that supports a blame culture, or has a strong command and control element, may find that the sharing of knowledge is limited. Weir and Hutchings (2005) suggest that knowledge cannot be understood outside of the cultural parameters that condition its emergence and modes of reproduction. Attitudes to knowledge sharing, as well as actual knowledge-sharing behaviour, depend on conditions that vary across institutional and cultural environments (Weir and Hutchings 2005). An ungrounded assumption is that people will share the knowledge they possess with others or tap into the collective corporate knowledge base in order to find a solution to problems simply because such systems have been made available (Sbarcea 2001 cited in Weir and Hutchings 2005). McDermott and O'Dell

(2001) discuss balancing the visible and invisible dimensions of culture, visibly by demonstrating the importance of sharing knowledge and building on the invisible core values. The idea that people will share knowledge openly in order to find a solution is not necessarily natural. Sharing is very much linked to collaborative aspects of the culture, and how those within the organisation operate together. Snowden (2000) argues that companies are gradually becoming aware that knowledge cannot be treated as an organisational asset without the active and voluntary participation of the communities that are its true owners. The main emphasis here is placed on the concept of the volunteer, rather than conscript, believing that a shift to considering employees as volunteers requires a radical rethink of the reward structure, organisational form and management attitude. The individual volunteering of information and knowledge links to the cultures arising within sections and departments within the organisation. Weir and Hutchings (2005) agree that the conditions under which individuals are prepared to share knowledge, either with other individuals or groups within the organisation, or with individuals or groups external to the organisation, differ between cultures. In particular, Von Krogh, Ichijo and Nonaka (2000) emphasise that the conditions for the creation of knowledge should include care, mutual trust and empathy. Their suggestion is that in order to share personal knowledge, individuals must rely on others to listen and react to their ideas. Thus, caring environments are important in a knowledge-focused organisation. Von Krogh et al. (2000) believe that constructive and helpful relations enable people to share their insights and freely discuss their concerns. Although culture is a strong fundamental element of knowledge management in its own right, it also forms part of the intellectual capital agenda. Human capital as part of intellectual capital is partly made up of cultural aspects within the context of the organisation.

A culture which supports the conditions specified by Von Krogh et al., including care, mutual trust and empathy, is at the heart of knowledge sharing, knowledge creation and innovation.

Summary

Communities (physical or virtual ones) are important mechanisms within the modern organisation and they can lead to innovative ideas and ultimately to change. In particular, virtual communities are becoming an important consideration in modern organisations. Making a decision about the design requirements for an online community and what features meet the organisational requirements is crucial, as is the need to be aware of generating social capital as the value added. This chapter has discussed types of communities that could be considered when designing for a virtual space. Understanding social capital concepts and how they can be developed in virtual communities enables an understanding of the potential of intangible value in the contemporary organisation. It has been suggested that the concept of social capital be extended to include ideas and intuition, which can be fully exploited by using web technologies. Ideas as currency may, therefore, form part of social capital generation, and lead to knowledge and innovation.

Providing a supportive culture for knowledge sharing and learning is particularly relevant because without a conducive culture, organisations may not be able to move forward effectively into the knowledge management domain. Assessing the organisational culture is important not only from a personal point view, but from a perspective of managing knowledge in the organisation. We have emphasised that knowledge sharing as part of knowledge creation operates within an open, caring, safe, trusting and collaborative culture and that culture forms part of an organisation's assets. Hence, it is important to realise that the sharing of knowledge and the practice of managing knowledge take place within the organisation depending upon the culture in place. Hence, initially identifying the cultural ethos and practice of an organisation or organisational department is a key condition for facilitating knowledge sharing. Ultimately an open environment encourages change and this leads to new ideas, creativity and innovation.

Reflective exercises

1. What types of community exist in your own organisation, and what makes them effective?

2. Are there any areas of interest that you have and that you feel so passionate about that you would consider establishing a community yourself within the organisation? In other words, could you take a bottom-up approach to forming a community of practice?

3. What factors in organisations encourage a *fear of sharing*?

4. What factors encourage a *trusting environment*?

5. Is the culture you work in caring, benign and supportive? Why or why not? In the knowledge-sharing company, why is this important?

10

Mobilising and designing the web infrastructure for twenty-first-century living

Abstract: This chapter highlights the tools and frameworks which may be useful in the web world by introducing a knowledge infrastructure and ecology. The chapter offers design readiness tools that could be useful to assess the principles that need to be considered when designing a knowledge-focused web environment.

Key words: knowledge infrastructure, knowledge ecology, design readiness assessment tool.

It is a new dawn. It is a new day – where technology dominates! We buy goods and services online, we follow courses and gain certificates in the virtual world. There has been a complete transformation in the way that we communicate and do business. We are dominated and influenced by technology at every level, from buying and selling to social networking. Social networking has become the norm for a whole new generation who use instant messaging, and the latest technological media for communication purposes. Today, the power of the blog reaches into all types of societies to sow many seeds of change. Technology has indeed become a very powerful tool with efficient, current, fast and smart features being used. These changes have been dramatic, occurring within a matter of years, rather than decades. These new killer applications supersede previous killer applications such as email. In this age of technology, wars are increasingly fought not only in the physical domain, but are fast becoming technological in nature. This arises both between corporate organisations and between nations. In this respect, we are of course back to the magic box as discussed in Chapter 8, because the only solution or resolution to be found may be through conversation and negotiation even if it is to be online. In other words, through peaceful means and respect for each other's positions, rather than through entrenched views. Of course, in this era, many businesses are using electronic forms of communicating to survive and to complement the current business model. The e-business model may be a transitional experiment for some organisations as they learn to navigate in a virtual world. However, with the rise of technology the corporate company may have no option but to embrace virtual forms of communicating.

We need to use the technology, but at the same time not be influenced to such an extent that we lose the ability to find answers within ourselves rather than without, or to lose sight of our integrity during the process. In the first section we discussed the importance of reflection as a means to re-evaluate personal accomplishments. The online tools enable us to use reflective features, and reflection leads to self-awareness. Therefore, it is important to make use of these features to work smarter and faster. Through reflection we can pause, rewind the tape, reconsider actions taken, and then re-evaluate our actions. By following this process, the professional can stop and change direction upon reflection. Without this capacity professionals may not be able to make judgements in retrospect about working practice. Any tool that is currently available to support this process may be very valuable. As already discussed, dialogue and conversation are a means to share knowledge and insight and develop new ideas. Managed conversation in web communities is of considerable value and is now at the heart of the web infrastructure. What is important in outer personal knowledge capital is putting value on those processes. This means being smart in the way you work and using the latest web technology.

Knowledge-based systems and value added

In the past, because of knowledge management's emergence from information sciences, the computational or technological paradigm has dominated the field. Many of the assumptions within this paradigm lead to a focus on systems, technology and modelling with the goal of optimising organisational knowledge management through the use of technology. In strategic terms, technology has expanded to become social, and thereby encompasses both codified distribution of knowledge and the generation of new knowledge creation through interactive social means.

Individual members of the organisation may wonder what can be achieved by focusing on knowledge creation and personal knowledge theory when designing web technologies. The answer lies in the potential to create more value added. In particular, it is the potential created by the new web technologies in the features that support interactive online activities which leads to the potential to exploit intellectual and social capital. In the current climate, exploiting these social tools enables the knowledge worker to interact more, which in turn leads to knowledge creation, learning and innovation. Therefore, in third generation knowledge management, designing for the exploitation of social capital is a requirement that can be exploited using knowledge-focused systems and the latest technology.

Knowledge and interactivity online

Knowledge workers do not work in isolation. Today they are supported by an organisational and ICT infrastructure where knowledge work can be handled more efficiently and effectively. They collaborate in teams, networks and communities and have to be supported by an adequate organisation and information and communication technological infrastructure. A knowledge management system (KMS) promises enhanced support for knowledge work through an integrated combination of information and communication technologies (Maier and Sametinger 2004). Virtual teams, expert networks, best practice groups and communities complement traditional organisational forms, such as work groups or project teams to aid collaboration between knowledge workers within, and increasingly across, organisations (Maier 2007). Personal Knowledge tools now encompass mobile technology, including smart phones, videos and i-pods which facilitate knowledge distribution and knowledge sharing. Taking advantage of the features, and the interoperability of tools, is at the heart of personal knowledge capital. However, it is the personalised aspects of the tools which make this aspect unique, because knowledge capital is all about self-management of personal knowledge. This is your decision in terms of working practice, and it allows for smart working practice and creative solutions.

The infrastructure and ecology for knowledge-based systems (IEKBS)

One of the effects of the interactive features arising in the new technologies is that they allow conversation and dialogue to flow either through synchronous (instant messaging) or non-synchronous (threaded discussion) methods in virtual space. As already discussed, this means that conversation is at the heart of any new infrastructure for knowledge creation. With this in mind, the author Young (2009) proposed an infrastructure for knowledge in her investigation of learning environments in education, which has been adapted for the corporate environment (see Figure 10.1 below).

The integrated layered knowledge infrastructure

Figure 10.1 shows a five-layered infrastructure. The layered knowledge infrastructure exploits tacit and explicit knowledge and utilises managed conversation. At the very heart of this knowledge infrastructure lies a circular tacit verse explicit element arising from the second level, and a managed conversational element at level four. The proposed

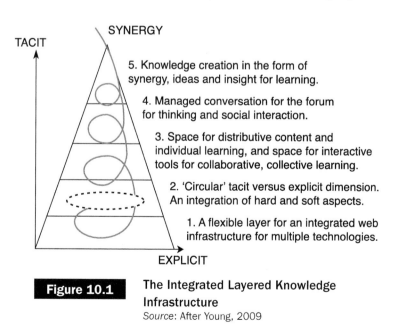

SYNERGY

TACIT

5. Knowledge creation in the form of synergy, ideas and insight for learning.

4. Managed conversation for the forum for thinking and social interaction.

3. Space for distributive content and individual learning, and space for interactive tools for collaborative, collective learning.

2. 'Circular' tacit versus explicit dimension. An integration of hard and soft aspects.

1. A flexible layer for an integrated web infrastructure for multiple technologies.

EXPLICIT

Figure 10.1 The Integrated Layered Knowledge Infrastructure
Source: After Young, 2009

infrastructure below differs significantly from a technical infrastructure approach as described by some writers, by focusing on the soft, tacit and collaborative elements for a knowledge-focused design. In particular, the Integrated Layered Knowledge Infrastructure creates a separate layer to incorporate a space for distributive content and individual learning, as well as a layer for use of interactive tools for collaborative, collective learning.

The knowledge infrastructure has been put forward for use in a context where there is a transition between both the codified aspects and the collaborative aspects of the technical infrastructure, both of which are appropriate for a learning environment. The first layer for a flexible integrated web environment is created with multi-layered integrated technologies in order to support a dynamic changing environment for connectivity. This layer uses enabling technologies: hybrid models, applications and devices supporting interoperability, mobile technology and cloud technology. This supports instant messaging, threaded discussion and repositories of knowledge to create a unified solution to maximise the benefits of technology and communications. This technical level supports the flexibility necessary to underpin a knowledge focused organisational infrastructure. This is followed by the second layer, a 'circular tacit versus explicit' dimension to emphasise the need to accommodate the soft and hard codified aspects of the web area that links to the SECI processes. The circular aspect links to the cyclical aspects of learning, and highlights the discrete nature of the tacit and explicit elements. The third layer provides for distributive content for individual learning and interactive tools for collaborative learning so that the design is for a combination of both elements. The distributive elements are found in the repository of knowledge or lessons learned for individualised learning, while the collaborative elements are linked to the interactive tools and apps supporting the social aspects of collective and collaborative learning. In other words, it creates space for the interactive online activity and space for codified knowledge repositories, and a whole range of other tools and apps that fall along this spectrum. The fourth layer of the infrastructure is designed to emphasise managed conversation where there are forums for thinking and social interaction to support the collaborative aspects of knowledge creation and collective learning. The tools and features to support the fourth level include interactive synchronous instant messaging and asynchronous threaded discussion forums. However, these spaces will not operate without a highly skilled champion or online moderator managing the website. The fifth layer of the process results in creating knowledge, which is predominantly focused on creating a synergy of ideas and insights.

This proposed tool is designed to aid sharing and creating knowledge in a collaborative manner, with special reference to the importance of the soft collaborative elements which are underpinned by the cyclical flow of tacit and explicit knowledge. In particular, the soft aspects focus on a space for dialogue and conversation for knowledge creation. However, any design of a knowledge-focused web infrastructure should highlight the managed conversational element while at the same time acknowledging the integrated hard and soft characteristics of the infrastructure, and the 'circular tacit versus explicit elements' that lead to knowledge creation as in Figure 10.1. The result is an infrastructure which is appropriate for those seeking to exploit intellectual and social capital. This creates an infrastructure for third generation knowledge management.

The ecological space for personal knowledge capital

The ecological space has been created for personal knowledge capital to support the growth of a virtual ecology for knowledge creation. Being able to take a conceptual overview of the design features required when creating a knowledge space is useful in the search to grasp the complexity of knowledge and the technologies in working practice. The design for an ecological space for collaborative knowledge (Figure 10.2) encompasses six features and provides a holistic perspective on the infrastructure space, and therefore covers every aspect and angle within the ecological globe. The ecological space builds on the infrastructure while focusing on the whole environment. Thus it presents an alternative perspective and view of the knowledge-focused learning environment. Six features make up the underlying ecology within the framework of Figure 10.2. The outer space around the structure shows the circular movement of the ecology, underpinned by a circular tacit-versus-explicit dimension, which is also represented by arrowed lines at the side. Feature (1) is supported by an individualised flexible integrated unified technical infrastructure. This is the backbone of the ecology. Feature (2) emphasises the need for both a physical and a virtual space where interaction can occur. This second feature also provides space for human experience online, where social interaction occurs through managed conversation within communities. Ultimately, the space (type of Ba) is like a classroom where ideas are thrown around and open to debate, so that learning and new knowledge arise. Feature (3) offers space for learning incorporating both distributive and collaborative elements. These elements comprise not only the infrastructure for explicit knowledge in the form of repositories of knowledge to generate re-usable memory and support individual learning, but also space for tacit-to-tacit interactivity. Feature (4) emphasises community, relationships and trust issues and supports the other features. The community aspect needs to be nurtured within any online space, and it is thus optimised by the relationships of the members of the community who interact and build trust between themselves. Feature (4) also demonstrates how a knowledge community eventually leads to the creation of a community of intelligence or wisdom: sharing a common mission and engaging in reflection and dialogue underpinned by trust, respect, care and empowerment. The community aspect is a vital component of the infrastructure and needs to be managed effectively by an online facilitator. Feature (5) allows for managed conversation and dialogue to arise within the community, in the virtual Ba space. Conversation and dialogue provide the context under which synergy arises within the online environment. This is the dynamic and interactive alive tacit environment alluded to within the literature. Dialogue and conversation are at the heart of knowledge creation and innovation, and they create synergy, knowledge and social capital. In particular, this space supports discursive media where conversation and dialogue may occur. These spaces support and facilitate knowledge sharing by providing the environment for online communities to flourish. The online space for dialogue and discussion of ideas, insight and reflection encourages dynamic interaction between individuals because online members can share each other's mental models, and possibly change their perceptions of reality. Feature (6) enables the flow of knowledge, which turns into a spiral of synergy and goes on to create new knowledge and innovative practice. You then have an ecology that will create social capital, knowledge creation and innovation. The circular tacit-versus-explicit dimension returns to the fundamental circular movement where tacit and explicit knowledge circulates, flows and moves between both the explicit repositories and back to the tacit interactive soft areas to be found in online space. The movement of the flow back and forward supports the transition between the static and dynamic areas, and supports the features mentioned above: resources; databases, lessons-learnt repository; artificial intelligence; search facilities; personal space; yellow pages; social media in the form of blogs and wikis; with email, instant messaging and threaded discussion moving in transition towards the other end of the spectrum. To sum up, what is required is the integration of these features so that

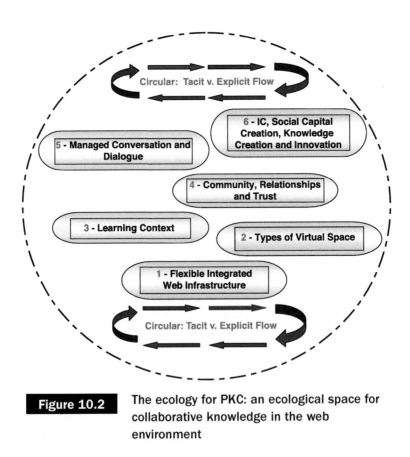

Figure 10.2 The ecology for PKC: an ecological space for collaborative knowledge in the web environment

knowledge flows between the various dimensions, and no one feature works alone, but all the levels integrate to permit knowledge to flow successfully around the environment created. Identifying the characteristics of an ecology to support the development of a knowledge creation and social capital flow through the web environment enables organisation members to make choices about what aspects they will need to use.

An assessment tool for designing a knowledge-focused web environment

The design readiness assessment tool (Table 10.1) was developed through theory, research and data analysis in order to examine the emergent design elements for a knowledge-focused web environment. Each part of the assessment tool relates to a particular element necessary when building this environment. The assessment tool was developed to help designers to see where they are in the process, and what elements and features and principles need to be developed in the future in order to create a knowledge-focused environment. The tool is designed to help the moderator understand the issues and details required to plan, prepare and design a knowledge-focused web environment.

The assessment tool outlines and proposes a set of principles that was derived from my own research using both empirical data and literature. Table 10.1 specifically focuses on knowledge management principles for interactive learning. Each principle includes the frameworks already discussed including Figures 10.1 and 10.2 above. The assessment tool supports a holistic and wide-ranging overview of principles that are necessary to consider when designing for a knowledge-focused web environment. In particular, the emphasis is on providing a list of necessary

Table 10.1 The design readiness assessment tool

Design Principle	Operationalised/Consequences; Example in Practice	Completed	Not completed	Comments
1 – Design for a Complex and Organic Ecology: Design for a **'Complex and Organic Environment'** which supports varying degrees of distribution elements and knowledge creation.	The array of software emerging continually becomes more advanced, and this has to form part of the technological infrastructure. In knowledge management terms, this complex environment has to incorporate space for the duality between the tacit and explicit knowledge elements of the design, which may include hard repositories for information and knowledge and soft areas where virtual interactive communities and social networking exist side by side. Future interoperability and unified solutions need to be taken into account.			
2 – Design for an Evolutionary Design: Design for a web environment for an **'Evolutionary'** design being created over time inclusive of feedback.	Continual feedback from users into the design of the tool helps the tool to continually co-evolve. This needs to be captured on a regular basis, and forms the bedrock of an evolutionary design process. An iterative design which supports student feedback from a prototype would be considered appropriate in this context.			

3 – Design for Integrated Unified Multiple Technologies: Design for the creation of a technical infrastructure to support 'integrated unified multiple technologies, tools and software across a variety of fields and disciplines (See Fig. 10.1 A Knowledge-Focused Web Infrastructure).	Example in practice: Using software that supports integrated technologies across its platform, and for multiple integrated features to emerge. This enables a complex array of tools and features to integrate within this environment to create a unified solution.
4 – Design for a Tacit v Explicit Cyclical Dimension: Design for an infrastructure to support and view a *'Tacit/Explicit Cyclical Dimension'* through a Knowledge Management lens (Fig 10.1)	The infrastructure supports the duality between the tacit and explicit dimension. This feature arises in a knowledge-focused infrastructure to include space for tacit and explicit interaction so that mechanisms exist for explicit knowledge stored in systems and space for online interactions via dialogue and conversational to emerge for knowledge creation and innovation. This encompasses the knowledge-focused web infrastructure frameworks. This may also become cyclical in nature and thereby link to the learning cycle in terms of continuous learning.

(Continued)

Table 10.1 The design readiness assessment tool (*Continued*)

5 – The Shamrock Leaf Metaphor: Design for the creation of a *'Shamrock Leaf'.* A metaphor which which blends places and spaces using mental, physical and virtual Ba (Nonaka, Toyama and Konno) and 'baby Ba' interactions, and a *'knowledge community'* (McDermott 1999a) of people in an environments where relationships, empathy and trust arise.	The Shamrock Leaf is a proposed metaphor which may be used when trying to understand knowledge creation within the learning environment (Young 2008). The Shamrock Leaf has three leaves. Each shamrock leaf is divided into two sections. The outer layer representing the mental, virtual and physical Ba, and the inner leaf representing the types of 'baby Ba' interactions taking place. The centre represents the 'community spirit', where the online moderator becomes the Gardener who oversees the growth of knowledge. This supports ba and community as a metaphor for 'blended aspects of learning'. This is a useful metaphor for moderators to grasp the fundamental issues involved.	
6 – Design for Distributive Knowledge and for Recycling of Individual Learning Design for the *'Recycling'* of lessons learnt, 'know-how', feedback, and activities.	This design principle links to learning aspects of the design, where elements of lessons learnt. The lessons learnt capability may be forged in the knowledge-repository on line where work and peer-to-peer presentations are stored. The recycling of know-how and feedback can be posted to the web environment for other s to use.	

7 – Design for a Caring, Benign and Safe Ecology: Design to create a *'Caring, Benign and Safe Environment'* to learn, share and be willing to recycle their knowledge.	There is an overlap between the need for a 'caring, benign and safe' environment to be created for learning to take place, and for knowledge creation to be fostered in education. Thus caring and benign environments suggest the fostering of love, and the safety element enables an open environment where ideas can be freely expressed (Von Krogh et al. 2000). This principle is also supported via the data analysis. Thus this principle derives from the literature review and data analysis both top-down and bottom-up. In knowledge creation learning occurs within a safe and caring environment.		
8 – Design for Knowledge Creation and Intellectual and Social Capital Creation: Design for the creation of value in the form of *'Social Capital'* assets arising from web activities.	A design element to make the moderator aware of the output of the design. This will arise as intangible elements are gleaned from online interactions, discussion and ideas and insight generated in the soft tacit features of the web. The outcome of these interactions may be valued in social capital terms. Reaching this level may also result in a high level of enthusiasm, engagement in the activities, increased collaborative activity, and the cohesion of the cohort.		

Table 10.1   The design readiness assessment tool *(Continued)*

9 – Design for a Gardener-Guide: Design for a 'Gardener, Guide' with the expertise and skill to manage, facilitate, energise and design knowledge-focused web ecology.	The online moderator provides the vision to design the tool, the energy and skill to facilitate the flow of knowledge and provides direction and guidance for the knowledge worker. The moderator as the gardener not only fosters and manages the growth of knowledge but motivates participants and thus provides a safe ecological environment for knowledge creation to foster. The moderator acts as a guiding star who needs to read the situation and facilitates the ba. The moderator needs the skills to manage both virtual and physical space.		

Source: after Young (2009)

steps that includes space for distribution and storage of knowledge and the creation of new knowledge creation; and focuses on third generation knowledge management where intellectual and social capital creation are highly valued. The intangible element is not a concept always considered, but the author believes that this concept needs to be raised to the forefront for future design features. These design frameworks will allow managers and online moderators to exploit elements including the tacit-versus-explicit elements; types of Ba; community; distributive and individual elements of learning; and social and intellectual capital. As discussed earlier, social and intellectual capital resides under the knowledge management umbrella, and is being brought to the forefront for consideration within this chapter.

Table 10.1 provides a pre-planning checklist for consideration by online moderators and designers who wish to set up a knowledge-focused web learning environment. The significance is that this tool gives the online moderator a framework to evaluate and consider the concepts required and the planning points necessary to set up and develop this type of environment. What is particularly important is that the tool has been designed to create a space to exploit the intangibles online.

Pruning the garden

So you have created your own garden, your own personal ecology, and now you need to think about how to keep the weeds out of the garden. Prune the weeds on a regular basis. This means deleting the information that is no longer relevant, that is outdated or surplus. Without pruning the information and knowledge ecology you have created, your tools and technologies will spill over and become a jungle of information overload. Therefore, prune on a regular basis, deleting the excess overload. In personal knowledge management, and in personal knowledge capital building, you have to take responsibility and be the gardener of your own assets. You have to identify and value those assets first, and then if you use technology you need to prune the garden by keeping the weeds at bay and not allow information overload to creep into your online repositories of information. You need to keep your online files up-to-date. You need to store and back-up the knowledge that is relevant to you, and prioritise your knowledge. Find your own way to do this suitable for your needs by pruning your own garden and creating your own technological environment.

In addition, it is imperative to be aware of online security. The lists of viruses continue to emerge daily, and not using appropriate security software is non-negotiable in this era. Always be aware of checking security sites when making online payment, and never leave behind in social networking personal information or dates, such as dates for engagements and weddings. Increasingly email has become highly sophisticated as it links to social networking sites and automatically makes many further links. Being on your guard is no bad thing; in fact, it is the way you have to operate within this era. Create your own ecology: be aware, be on your guard, because you need to work your ecology to your advantage.

Summary

It is the business of the knowledge worker to exploit the web tools to the best of their ability for swift knowledge-sharing purposes, reflection and collective distribution. In outer knowledge capital valuing ideas, insight and know-how are highly valued, and can ultimately be developed by facilitating and exploiting the new web technologies. Careful consideration of the design principles necessary to exploit third generation knowledge tools is imperative, and two frameworks have been proposed in the form of the Integrated Layered Knowledge Infrastructure (Figure 10.1) and the Knowledge Ecology (Figure 10.2). Finally, a checklist for design principles has been proposed. Table 10.1 provides the steps on how to design environments that exploit the web environment for third generation knowledge management. These tools and frameworks place value on the development of social capital in relation to the advancement of new web technologies.

Reflective exercises

1. What tools do you use to create knowledge for yourself which you will then distribute to colleagues?
2. Which are the tools that specifically help you to reflect?
3. What part do you think conversation plays online, in terms of creating value for yourself and the company?
4. How often do you prune the personal 'technological ecologies' you have created?
5. How do you protect yourself online? What mechanisms have you in place, and what practice and principles do you operate to do this?
6. From the tools outlined, which elements do you consider to be crucial when designing a knowledge-focused web environment?

11

The application and exploration of knowledge creation theory

Abstract: How do we develop knowledge creation in the virtual environment? This chapter examines and explores knowledge creation by focusing on the Unified Model of Knowledge Creation. Nonaka and Takeuchi (1995) originally discussed the SECI model at the heart of knowledge creation and this model was further expanded by Nonaka, Toyama and Konno (2000) by introducing Ba, KCAs and the management of the process.

Key words: the Unified Model of Knowledge Creation, Ba, knowledge creation assets, managing online facilitation.

At the present time, organisational knowledge has acquired a new status. Corporate businesses who wish to become competitive contemporary organisations without resorting to outdated methods should rethink their approach and become knowledge-focused by endeavouring to value intangible knowledge. This chapter will examine some of the outcomes from my own applied research into knowledge creation and the web environment, where I used both the Unified Model of Knowledge Creation theory presented by Nonaka et al. (2000) and grounded theory to examine the data. This chapter incorporates a broad overview of knowledge creation processes and how this relates to the contemporary learning environment. This chapter and the next show the outcome of this research.

The Unified Model of Knowledge Creation

At the heart of all knowledge management thinking are the processes of knowledge creation outlined by Nonaka and Takeuchi (1995) in the SECI model, and further developed by Nonaka, Toyama and Konno (2000). Nonaka et al. (2000) addressed the criticism of being overly simplistic in the SECI model, by extending the model into a more complex study of knowledge creation. What matters is how this model relates to personal knowledge. This is particularly crucial as we move into an era where the knowledge worker is operating within both virtual and physical space. How the model impacts and helps us understand the interactions and processes to be adopted may help us to understand the theory as it relates to learning. Building on the early SECI

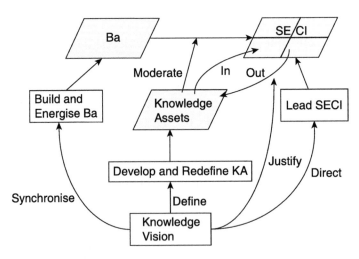

Figure 11.1 The Unified Model of Knowledge Creation
Source: Reproduced with permission from Elsevier, from Nonaka, Toyama and Konno (2000) 'Seci, Ba and Leadership: a Unified Model of Dynamic Knowledge Creation' in *Long Range Planning 33:* pp5–34.

model of Nonaka (1991) and Nonaka and Takeuchi (1995), the Unified Model of Knowledge Creation (Nonaka, Toyama and Konno, 2000) has four main elements which include the original SECI model; the Knowledge Creation Assets; types of Ba; and the leadership and energy issues. The model is suitable for physical as well as virtual media, which is very useful because we are rapidly moving towards a virtual interactive mode of collaboration with the arrival of new web tools and technologies. In the unified model in Figure 11.1 all the elements within the flow lead back to the SECI processes.

The SECI model

At the centre of the unified model is the original SECI model of knowledge creation that shows the interactions and synergy between tacit and explicit processes. As discussed earlier, it is within the socialisation process of the early SECI model that individual tacit-to-tacit knowledge starts life. The interactions between tacit and explicit knowledge lead to knowledge creating processes occurring. The SECI model highlights the tacit versus explicit dimension, and shows the individual as the starting point for knowledge creation processes. Within the SECI model, organisational knowledge creation processes are a spiral process starting at the individual level and moving up through expanding communities of interaction which cross sectional, departmental, divisional and organisational boundaries. A swirl of creativity and energy emerges as the synergy is released and the interactive processes occur.

The changing nature of the Ba metaphor

A dimension within the Unified Model of Knowledge Creation is the Ba. The Japanese concept of Ba which roughly translates as 'place', was originally proposed by Kitaro Nishida (1921, 1970) and Hiroshi Shimizu (1995), and has been adapted by Nonaka and Konno (1998). Nonaka and Konno (1998) argue that Ba is a shared space that provides a platform for advancing individual and collective knowledge and acts as a foundation for knowledge creation. Organisational context can be physical, virtual or mental (existential), or all three. Ba is conceived as the frame (made up of the borders of space and time) in which knowledge is activated as a resource for knowledge creation where it is intangible, boundaryless and dynamic. Nonaka, Toyama and Konno (2000) argue that value creation in knowledge-creating companies arises from the interactions within the shared Ba, and emphasise that these interactions can be valued as a resource concentration for knowledge assets and intellectual capabilities. Moreover, Nonaka and Konno (1998) state that according to the theory of existentialism, Ba is a context, which 'harbours meaning', suggesting that Ba is a 'shared space' that serves as a foundation for knowledge creation, and grounds the concept of Ba within an existentialist framework. In introducing the idea of Ba as a mechanism for knowledge creation, Nonaka and Konno (1998) emphasise that Ba may exist at many levels, which connect to form a greater Ba (known as Basho). The Ba expand and interact within and between each other to form a Basho or greater Ba. In this respect the Ba provide a platform for the process of knowledge creation. An example of Ba in everyday life is shown in Figure 11.2 below. The Ba space may be inside the knowledge worker's head; it is the physical

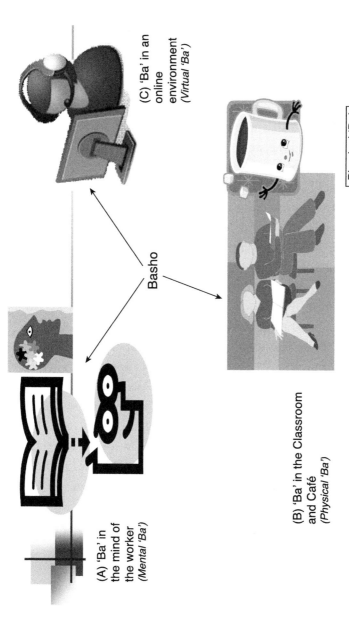

(A) 'Ba' in the mind of the worker (Mental 'Ba')

(B) 'Ba' in the Classroom and Café (Physical 'Ba')

(C) 'Ba' in an online environment (Virtual 'Ba')

Basho

Physical 'Ba'

Figure 11.2 Visualisation of the Ba and Basho
Source: After Young 2009b.
Image used with permission from Microsoft

space in the meeting room or work café and it is the virtual space in the online community in the workplace.

The Ba can be viewed as a type of metaphor for places and spaces in which we reach out, develop, and interact with one another. As knowledge creation evolves it does so within the boundaries of Ba according to this theory. An easy way to remember Ba is to think of it in the form of a shamrock leaf. The petals of the shamrock stand for the mental, physical or virtual space and the stem can be viewed as the gardener who orchestrates the symphony between these three spaces. Nonaka and Konno (1998) emphasise that the characteristics of Ba are loosely linked to the SECI processes. In this respect, socialisation is linked to 'Originating Ba' which is face-to-face; externalisation is linked to 'Interacting Ba' which is peer-to-peer; 'Cyber Ba' is linked to combination which is group-to-group activity, and 'Exercising Ba' is linked to Internalisation. Nonaka and Konno (1998) suggest that the organic concentration of knowledge assets in Ba involves an *ecological process* within a cyclical cultivation of resources, suggesting that knowledge creation and its application are an ecology, not an economy, and that 'Ba is the stage' for this resource cycle. From the point of view of the Unified Model of Knowledge Creation, Ba represents the stage and the ecological space where knowledge creation is enacted. It is the ecological and flexible dimensions of the Ba that make it attractive as a place or space for knowledge creation.

'Ba', changing labels, and virtual interaction

The labels used to describe the 'types of Ba' in Nonaka's work have developed and changed over time, resulting in some variance in the interpretation of these labels used for Ba. In Nonaka and Konno's (1998) earlier work the label for face-to-face collective interaction was 'Interacting Ba', and in Nonaka, Toyama and Konno's (2000) paper the face-to-face collective element became 'Dialoguing Ba'. All well and good, but what about virtual dialoguing Ba? The assumption is that dialogue only occurs in a face-to-face environment, when in fact today, virtual dialogue occurs in most social media. Moreover, in their earlier work Nonaka and Konno (1998) discuss a 'Cyber Ba' label which, as it happens, is virtual and collective, while in the later work by Nonaka, Toyama and Konno (2000) this label changes to 'Systemising Ba' which is also virtual and collective, and clearly suggests a space for the synthesis of explicit-to-explicit documents. It is clear from Nonaka's work that the model of knowledge creation has developed over time, and that this is evidenced from the changing Ba sub-labels being used. However, the changes in the labels have not kept pace with the changes occurring in technology, and in particular with reference to the interactive media. Not only is there confusion about the Ba labels and their meaning, but consideration needs to be given to identifying the space where the virtual interactive elements of conversation and dialogue occur within the Ba. Thus, where should we position the virtual space for online dialogue and discussion to take place in light of the arrival of technologies which have tools for interactive elements? In essence, the Ba labels do not overtly and clearly highlight where the interactive virtual discursive elements arise, that can support discursive media. This leaves the Ba open to interpretation. This situation is relevant to a corporate context, because understanding and identifying where the physical and virtual interactive place and space exists in the company is vital. The above discussion on the Ba as a representation of an existential, physical and virtual pictorial metaphor is useful, and this can be further illustrated in the idea of the shamrock leaf. Moreover, Ba as a context for the emergence of interactions and conversation leading to

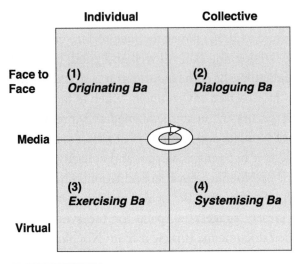

	Individual	Collective
Face to Face	(1) *Originating Ba*	(2) *Dialoguing Ba*
Media		
Virtual	(3) *Exercising Ba*	(4) *Systemising Ba*

Figure 11.3 Four types of Ba

Source: Reproduced with permission from Elsevier, from Nonaka, Toyama and Konno (2000) 'Seci, Ba and Leadership: a Unified Model of Dynamic Knowledge Creation' in *Long Range Planning 33:* pp5–34.

newly developed ideas and insight may be valued in terms of a space to develop social capital. This is the 'value added' for the organisation which cares to identify the intangible nature of knowledge creation. The comparison between the four Ba outlined by Nonaka, Toyama and Konno (2000) is illustrated in Figure 11.3.

Valuing Knowledge Creation Assets (KCAs)

All the assets of an organisation are valuable, whether tangible or intangible. Understandably, identifying intangible assets is not always easy, but it is imperative to do so in the twenty-first-century organisation. In the Unified Model of Knowledge Creation Nonaka et al. (2000) have introduced the concept of the Knowledge Creation Assets (KCAs). The assumption is that identifying these intangible assets will lead to greater levels of value added for the organisation. However, identifying the Knowledge Creation Assets may be a complex process. The use of the asset language implies a link with intangible aspects and, in particular, with intellectual capital, so that intellectual capital is somehow part of the knowledge creation process. Nonaka, et al. (2000) define assets as 'firm-specific resources that are indispensable to create value for the firm'. They suggest that trust among organisational members is created as an output in the knowledge creating process. This suggests that although knowledge is considered to be one of the most important assets for a firm to create a sustainable competitive advantage, we do not always have an effective system and tools for evaluating and managing Knowledge Creation Assets. Nonaka et al. (2000) emphasise that existing accounting systems are inadequate for capturing the value of knowledge assets, and that due to the tacit nature of knowledge this suggests that the knowledge assets must be uniquely built, identified and used internally in order for their full value to be realised. In the unified model the KCAs are sub-divided into four parts. The *experiential knowledge assets* suggest a type of learning in action approach; *conceptual knowledge assets* can be linked to images, symbols, and language and may be a part of brand equity; *routine knowledge assets* may be part of the routine practices and cultural dimension within the context of the organisation; and *systemic knowledge assets* relate to stored and packaged knowledge content.

The application of Knowledge Creation Assets in virtual space

The KCAs represent the inputs and outputs of the complex knowledge creation process. However, it needs to be acknowledged that these inputs and outputs are not clearly identified within the unified theory, and are therefore open to interpretation. Identifying the inputs and outputs in the knowledge creation process within a specific context is crucial to understanding this process, and more evidence is required to enable the clear identification of the KCAs. The author's own research investigation identified the KCAs within an online virtual environment in education and this gave a hint as to how these assets arise in practice. In particular, when the KCA theory was applied to the data the output revealed that *conceptual* knowledge assets were viewed as part of the web design where, in this instance, the website acted as a guide for student learning to take place. *Experiential* assets are tacit and difficult to grasp, evaluate or trade. They include skills and know-how acquired through experience. Within the study, experiential knowledge assets were the learning processes taking place online including shared common experiences, learning by doing, comparing and contrasting, learning from mistakes, and gaining insight, skills and knowledge acquired from the website. In fact, they add sustainable competitive advantage. Four sub-areas of experiential knowledge assets not found include emotional knowledge, physical knowledge, energetic knowledge and rhythmic knowledge. It was because these areas need further research that the author decided to examine emotional knowledge in more detail as shown in the first section. Indeed, in this book, emotional knowledge assets as part of experiential knowledge assets can be viewed as part of the LOFT model. The *routine* knowledge assets were perceived habits and organisational routines taking place particularly in the workplace, which in this specific instance were embedded in email practices. Finally, the *systemic* knowledge assets were the visible parts of the website where systemised packaged knowledge was visibly displayed. By applying the KCA theory in a practical manner to an online context, the results help us to understand how the Knowledge Creation Assets occur.

The management of the knowledge creation theory

So far the discussion has centred on the knowledge creation process, but it is the management of this process which supports the creation of knowledge. This is the fourth aspect supporting knowledge creation in the unified model. To support this process a *moderator/director/facilitator* is required, whose role is to cross-fertilise the knowledge creation flow. The need for effective management forms part of the management of knowledge creation itself. In this respect, the nature, characteristics and skills of the facilitator are crucial to the development of energy and synergy, which in turn will lead to knowledge creation, insight and innovation. A moderator's awareness of tacit knowledge and his/her ability to facilitate intangible value is vital to the success of a knowledge-focused web environment. Good management of the Ba is crucial. Energy arising within the Ba, and the moderator's ability to read and manage the Ba situation, becomes an important element in the success or failure of Ba and Basho. Moderators have to facilitate the interactions to create energy among participants within the various Ba, and among the participants based on the moderator's vision. This implies that energy is facilitated by a moderator whose skill is central to the knowledge creation process and leads to a Basho of swirling dynamic energy. This management process supports the proposition that the moderator/director/facilitator must be consciously aware of mobilising powerful forces in the Ba space to support emerging processes with visionary proposals, skill, commitment, craft and the personal commitment of time.

Managing the virtual environment

The moderator's role is crucial to successful discursive media within an online virtual environment. Managing conversation is a key aspect of managing the knowledge creation process. It is the skill of the online moderator to manage the conversation which is imperative within organisations. Von Krogh et al. (2000) argue that good conversations are the cradle of social knowledge. They argue that extended discussion can encompass personal flights of fancy as well as careful exposition of ideas. In this respect, people's participation in conversation means exploring new ideas and reflecting on other people's viewpoints, via the mutual exchange of ideas, viewpoints and beliefs that conversation entails. Underlying this managed conversational dimension are the individual and group exchanges, the openness to ideas, and the culture and trust created. When members of an organisation trust one another, creativity is encouraged, and even playfulness. At a deeper level, the implication here is that there is a reliance on a new sense of empathy, sensitivity and care in the organisation, which highlights how people treat each other and encourages creativity and even playfulness. The moderator, whether in the form of manager or moderator of knowledge creation, needs to be aware of the intangible nature of tacit knowledge, and have the skills to manage conversation through physical and virtual interactions. The facilitator, therefore, needs to identify the Ba space rapidly, and be aware of the processes for knowledge creation, including those that occur at the individual level. With all these skills the moderator/director/facilitator then becomes a creator, designer, leader and gardener.

Table 11.1   Managing the virtual knowledge environment

The online director acts as: director	Provides vision within the learning environment
Middle manager, moderator and facilitator	Identifies and manages the emerging Bas in mental (existential) individual, physical (classroom) or virtual (web) situations.
Guiding star – (guide)	Awareness and ability to read the situation and to connect to the various Ba.
Requires the skill to manage both a virtual and physical space in a learning environment	■ Designs web and directs the virtual Ba ■ Enables organic development of website from feedback by using iterative design ■ Recycles resources, with the creation of a knowledge resource. Manages the resources ■ Cultivates a benign climate for knowledge creation and learning, which includes comfort and safety factors. Creates a safe learning environment ■ Breaks down barriers early on ■ Manages and facilitates conversation ■ Acts as a facilitator of knowledge creation and learning ■ Energises and stokes the fire within the Ba ■ Removes redundant information on the web – by acting as a gardener

Source: After Young (2009)

Skills of facilitation rather than control, high levels of energy, and a caring nature may all contribute to the success of a managed knowledge creation environment. Individual members within the organisation inevitably have an ability to enhance or restrict the flow of knowledge throughout the organisation, although they may also set up barriers to restrict this flow. A culture that emphasises innovation, care, a knowledge-sharing mentality and is supportive of core business processes, sophisticated IT and cyber Ba allows knowledge to flow. Management of the process facilitates both continuity and innovation. The author's (Young 2009) educational investigation into the characteristics necessary for a manager within the virtual environment is summed up in Table 11.1 above. It shows that the tutor acts as a guide and provides the vision. They act as middle managers who identify the Ba weaving in and out of virtual and physical space. They become adept at reading situations and as such are looked upon as guiding stars. With practice, moderators acquire the skills to design, direct and develop the virtual Ba, creating iterative feedback and recycling content and resources.

They become like the gardener of the resource by regularly removing redundant information and they create a benign safe climate for learning, breaking down barriers early in the learning experience. They act as a facilitator of knowledge creation by stoking the fire, creating challenges and stirring up new and exciting developments when required. In this way, being a director/moderator/guide/facilitator/gardener/web designer are all roles that may be required when creating a dynamic and interactive virtual learning environment for knowledge creation.

Summary

The Unified Model of Knowledge Creation is a fully comprehensive model which emphasises not only the SECI processes but the need for a Ba, valuing Knowledge Creation

Assets (KCAs) and the management of this process. Because of the nature of this model it has become essential to understand how it operates in a virtual environment. The placement of a virtual interactive Ba has therefore been explored. However, it is the management of the Ba which sharply makes the difference in terms of successful knowledge creation, and this process will depend on the style and skill of the moderator. We need to understand this role and how it will impact on the knowledge creation process, whether in the physical or virtual environment. The director as a moderator and facilitator will need to understand the issues relating to managing this context in terms of their intent, vision, and desire to create a safe and fun environment using managed conversation for knowledge creation. The nature, characteristics and skill required for this role in the knowledge creation context are crucial for success. The next chapter will focus on further developing the unified theory of knowledge creation in a web-world.

Reflective exercises

1. What are the main elements within the Unified Model of Knowledge Creation? Why are they so important?

2. What makes moderation so crucial in a virtual environment? What skills and traits does the virtual moderator need to have and why?

3. In what way was the unified model extended in the (inner path) section, and why?

12

The Knowledge Cube: a model for knowledge creation in the web environment

Abstract: It is hard to visualise all of the processes necessary when trying to develop knowledge creation in a virtual environment. The Knowledge Cube is a visual representation of processes required in a web world. The Knowledge Cube is particularly aimed at the knowledge worker who wishes to create, design and understand virtual knowledge creation processes that lead to innovative practice.

Key words: the Knowledge Cube model, personal knowledge capital, inner and outer path of knowledge creation.

Personal knowledge creation is suitable for those managers and knowledge workers who wish to dig deep for answers, not just rely on external props, but rather believe in placing value on intangibles, not just on tangibles. So far we have highlighted the importance of intangible value, discussed Ba and KCAs, and the management and characteristics necessary for leadership of the virtual space, and introduced the Ka (*personal inner knowledge*) to the SECI model of knowledge creation. We have also examined the tools and technologies for the knowledge worker, offered an integrated infrastructure and ecology for knowledge creation, and discussed relationships, trust and culture as extremely important to *outer personal knowledge creation*. All of this supports creating an environment for the power of ideas.

The Knowledge Cube processes

The author has integrated the ideas, concepts, models and frameworks introduced in previous chapters to introduce the Knowledge Cube as a proposed adapted model for virtual knowledge creation. The Knowledge Cube (Figure 12.1) brings together all the strands previously discussed and is a model generated as a metaphor for knowledge creation in virtual space. This is an adaptation of Nonaka, Toyama and Konno's (2000) Unified Model of Knowledge Creation. The Cube has been created as a way of communicating a complex set of ideas. This framework extends to discussing four elements of knowledge creation, namely: SECI, Ba, knowledge assets, and the management aspects to create the four sides of the cube. The Cube, therefore, extends to four elements rather than three elements as in Nonaka et al. (2000). The Cube is supported by the flow of knowledge and ideas circulating from top to bottom in the cube.

The first Knowledge Cube (Young 2009) was developed from my own earlier research investigation, to provide a metaphor and framework for tutors in higher education. My investigation enabled an in-depth examination of the web environment through the lens of knowledge management and knowledge creation theory. This Knowledge Cube has been adapted for a corporate environment and shows an over-arching and fully comprehensive view of the requirements (conceptual and practical) necessary for business professionals to develop a knowledge-focused web environment. The Knowledge Cube emphasises the over-arching elements and issues for knowledge creation, highlighting virtual interactive space, infrastructure, culture, community and type of management. The Knowledge Cube is unique in that it gives a wider view of the areas and issues necessary to design and plan for the virtual space. The proposed Knowledge Cube produces a high-level overview of the reasoning and thinking necessary to plan. Above all, frameworks, models and tools show the detail on how to prepare, design and develop for a knowledge-focused website. The focus is to create and design web environments which exploit web technologies for third generation knowledge management to incorporate community and social and intellectual capital while highlighting ideas as a form of currency.

The aim of the knowledge-focused web environment should be to build and design a space to encompass a broader learning base where there is 'space for both thinking and for the storage of knowledge and information', thereby creating a 'human centred' knowledge system. The Knowledge Cube sits on two layers which are imperative for creating knowledge in a virtual environment. The four sides of the cube are made up of the four original elements in the unified model: the SECI; Ba; KCAs and management of the web. The SECI now extends to include Ka as discussed in Chapter 5.

Layer one of the Cube

The integrated web infrastructure layer (1) of the Cube supports the enabling technology for a virtual environment. The first layer incorporates The Layered Knowledge Infrastructure (Figure 10.1). In particular, the system would incorporate designing for a complex organic ecology that needs to grow and develop along with the latest available technologies. The design includes a socio-technical infrastructure to support static, codified, explicit and distributive aspects, as well as the tacit, interactive, dynamic, collaborative, collective conversational elements. The integrated unified infrastructure would then support inter-operability with a whole array of other technological and communication devices for mobile and flexible working. It would include a repository of knowledge, and have space for online interactions (instant messaging and threaded discussion) and thereby provide for both the distribution of knowledge and the creation of new knowledge. In particular, providing an infrastructure to support managed conversation aspects of design is imperative for learning and interacting online especially in an era where the tools are available to do so. The integrated infrastructure would support space for the cyclical aspects of knowledge to emerge on a continuum between tacit and explicit knowledge. An iterative design for the human feedback underpins the system and is fundamental to the success of any knowledge system, and the interplay between knowledge creation and distribution becomes imperative.

Layer two of the Cube

The community, culture and learning context layer (2a and b) helps create a learning environment to support the Knowledge Cube. It is desirable to create a benign climate which lends itself to being part of a homely environment. This benign culture is created within an online community and learning space where the individual does not feel threatened or intimidated by online activity, but instead feels safe, comfortable and cared for. In this way, within the community, knowledge workers are free and open to learning by making mistakes. Without this safe and caring environment, interactivity, learning and sharing are unlikely to take place. This second layer therefore incorporates a safe learning environment within the knowledge community, where learning and discussion can take place. Thus, the moderator of the community can create an environment for the creation of knowledge through social capital generation.

At the centre are collaborative and trusting relationships. It is the development of these relationships which helps to create knowledge creating processes.

The Cube

(A) is the knowledge worker who participates in the process, and (B) is the energy arising from this activity. The management of the process (C) is supported by the moderator as a director, designer and facilitator of the environment, community and culture in which they find themselves. The moderator creates the vision, manages the design of the web environment and acts as the facilitator and gardener of this environment. Their role is highly significant to the success or failure of this virtual environment. This is captured above in Table 10.1.

Within the Knowledge Cube are the four main categories of knowledge creation. This includes the SECI (D): socialisation, externalisation, combination and internalisation reside at the back of the cube. The SECI is now extended to include Ka and Co-Ka and the LOFT model. At the front of the cube we see the Knowledge Creation Assets (KCAs) (E), where the heart represents the value at the centre. Identifying where the KCAs currently reside is invaluable to the organisation as this highlights the areas where intangible value lies In particular, it helps enormously if management understand that the valued outputs from the learning processes are, in fact, based on perception of reality and practice.

The four Ba categories supporting the mental, virtual and physical space reside at the side of the cube in Figure 12.1. To address the question of where the virtual interactive elements of the Ba reside, the Ba (F) itself has been modified to include both a (3a) 'virtual systemising' and (3b) 'virtual discursive' space. This represents space for downloading

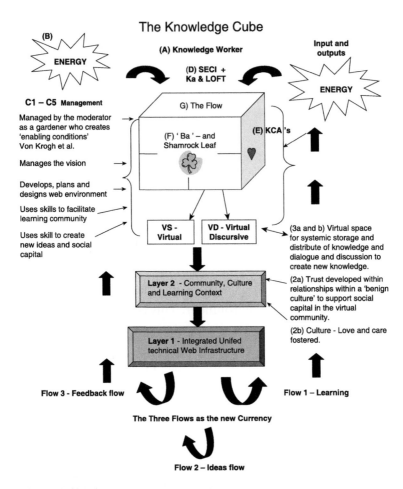

The Knowledge Cube

(B) ENERGY

(A) Knowledge Worker

Input and outputs

(D) SECI + Ka & LOFT

ENERGY

C1 – C5 Management

Managed by the moderator as a gardener who creates 'enabling conditions' Von Krogh et al.

Manages the vision

Develops, plans and designs web environment

Uses skills to facilitate learning community

Uses skill to create new ideas and social capital

G) The Flow

(F) ' Ba ' – and Shamrock Leaf

(E) KCA 's

VS - Virtual

VD - Virtual Discursive

(3a and b) Virtual space for systemic storage and distribute of knowledge and dialogue and discussion to create new knowledge.

Layer 2 - Community, Culture and Learning Context

(2a) Trust developed within relationships within a 'benign culture' to support social capital in the virtual community.

Layer 1 - Integrated Unifed technical Web Infrastructure

(2b) Culture - Love and care fostered.

Flow 3 - Feedback flow

Flow 1 – Learning

The Three Flows as the new Currency

Flow 2 – Ideas flow

Figure 12.1   The Knowledge Cube for knowledge creation within the virtual environment (After Young 2009)

from the knowledge repository, as well as space for virtual interactions in the form of dialogue and discussion. At the heart of the Ba is a Shamrock Leaf that is a metaphor to represent the three parts of the Ba: mental, physical and virtual. The shamrock has a stem that represents the moderator as the gardener who sustains the interactions among the various spaces. Overall the Ba itself supports a

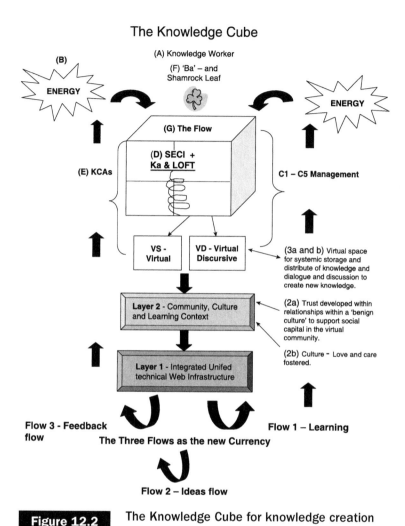

Figure 12.2 The Knowledge Cube for knowledge creation within the virtual environment: side view (After Young 2009)

suitable physical and virtual environment for 'blended learning' in the dynamic workplace. The outcomes flowing through the cube include the cyclical flow, learning processes flow and ideas flow, all forming the basis of the three flows as shown in the Cube. The first flow is to the knowledge repository within the website, and represents the learning processes that were occurring as the knowledge worker individually interacted peer-to-peer with the web resource. This space creates a cyclical aspect in the recycling of work. These learning processes emphasise the facilitation skills being used that resulted in comparing and contrasting standards, skills and know-how; reflecting on learning and creating new ideas, hints, tips and insight. The second flow is the ideas flow resulting from the use of 'interactive space' created for conversation and dialogue through threaded discussion and live chat features. In particular, the process of creating ideas, insight, and hints and tips from both the repository and interactive parts of the website form the new currency within the virtual environment. The third flow is the feedback flow from the user (the knowledge worker in this case), about the design and development of the website. The three flows underpin the processes and activities resulting from creating a knowledge-focused web environment. The three flows form part of the inputs and outputs in knowledge creation.

Summary

The Knowledge Cube contributes to an over-arching and comprehensive view of knowledge creation activity and provides a metaphor and a detailed overview for the corporate sector to grasp the strategic fundamental issues, the concepts, and the rethinking necessary to embark on creating online knowledge. The Knowledge Cube is particularly aimed at the knowledge worker who wishes to create, design and understand virtual knowledge creation processes that lead to innovative practice. Building on the work of Nonaka et al. (2000), the model presented is suitable for the virtual environment for knowledge creation. In so doing, it has the advantage of being supported by two layers, one supporting a technical infrastructure and one supporting a conducive culture for knowledge to flourish. By using the Knowledge Cube model in this way, the smart knowledge worker has a number of factors that they can instantly bring into play when wanting to create new knowledge. Creating the Cube metaphor enables this process to be more easily understood.

Conclusion:
the inner and outer path
of knowledge creation

Knowledge capital as part of knowledge creation combines an inner and outer path for the knowledge worker. Outer knowledge capital examines web technologies to facilitate and create knowledge and exploit intangibles. Inner knowledge capital, as part of an inner path, examines know-how from a deep personal awareness level. Inner and outer knowledge capital can be explored and exploited by individual knowledge workers in order to make their working lives more productive and satisfying as they maximise their own skills, awareness and tools. In particular, the inner and outer path of knowledge creation tries to re-address the imbalance that has occurred where technology dominates to the extent that individuals become subservient to meaning derived from the new modes of communication. In a world where there is so much focus on the web technologies and web environment for everyday communication, perhaps it is time to re-address the imbalance and go within. This is a world where science and technology are beginning to dominate but where our own true nature will in fact lead us to the real wisdom available. To re-address the imbalance that has begun to occur, and to make for a more balanced approach, personal knowledge capital has introduced The inner path of knowledge creation in order to tap into creative forces that align to our greater selves. Table 13.1 displays the format for the inner and outer personal knowledge capital.

Inner personal knowledge capital

The whole concept of knowledge capital helps to bring to the fore an intuitive and inner path, which until now has not been viewed as mainstream within the corporate organisation. Due to the increasing demands in the work environment the busy knowledge worker may well need to create balance by taking some quiet time out to meditate, create mindfulness space, exercise, walk, and even laugh in order to get back to being and self. Personal knowledge capital contributes by encouraging knowledge workers to take this first step to access their deep knowing at the individual level. Quiet Zen time allows us to introspect and get in touch with self, and in this way, we can use our inner self to help us navigate through life. Going inwards is part of a type of inner technology, which helps the individual to keep a balance between the inner and outer world in which we reside. Retreating to the inner world enables the individual to go into themselves to listen to inner self in order to find solutions appropriate to their own unique abilities. In other words, the wisdom is within! It is up to the knowledge worker to create their own environment for personal knowledge capital. Being 'aware' of the importance of the innate 'inner' assets you have enables you to take control of your own destiny and drive into a future that you have managed and created. You need to value your own self-worth, and by doing so create a benchmark for yourself by which to live. The personal knowledge capital approach supports the view that the individual's intuitive greater self can also be used for personal and corporate awareness. In other words, developing the

'Ka' within the theory of knowledge creation allows knowledge workers to value their own intangible assets, albeit those which are difficult to define. Mastering self can be cultivated by focusing on the tacit cognitive aspects of the mind through observation of self-talk. In this way the knowledge worker is encouraged to take responsibility and develop themselves personally. This process complements a rational view in the business environment to include intuitive individual processes, so that this practice becomes a trait of the true professional. The concept of personal knowledge capital encompasses the realm of knowledge creation, including emotional knowledge within the socialisation process of the SECI model, and emotional knowledge assets within experiential Knowledge Creation Assets. The author proposes the extension of knowledge creation dimensions to include not only a technical and cognitive dimension but a new personal awareness dimension. Chapter 5 takes personal knowledge to the next level by creating the Knowledge Awareness Model of Knowledge Creation (The LOFT). The LOFT model extends the SECI model of knowledge creation into personal awareness. In doing so, knowledge awareness (Ka) emerges as deep individual personalised knowledge. Added to this, the LOFT and Ka extend SECI in the Knowledge Cube model.

The outer path of personal knowledge capital

External personal knowledge capital comprises identifying and valuing social capital within networks, physical and virtual communities and the culture in which you find yourself. The outer path to personal knowledge capital highlights how the professional knowledge worker can make best use of their social and intellectual capital by managing the networks of relationships created, and the technology on offer. Awareness of the subtle force of trusting relationships within a business context and within the organisation team becomes imperative for open communication for external knowledge capital. The outer path of personal knowledge capital encourages you to manage your own assets through the communities and networks you interact with, as you exploit the latest technologies around you. It enables you to value the 'intangible', rather than focus only on the tangibles in the business environment. The intangibles create and enable subtle changes to take place.

Balancing, valuing and exploiting your personal knowledge capital

In most cases, it is intangible value that leads to new insight and ideas, and higher levels of creative and innovative thinking. In this process, value is placed on ideas as a currency. Using interactive virtual web tools helps the knowledge worker to organise their own thoughts, self-reflect, share ideas and insights with others and modify their 'mental footprint' in order to positively move forward. Because of this, design for a technical knowledge-focused infrastructure includes conversation and dialogue and a tacit/explicit continuum. An infrastructure, ecology and design checklist have been presented to help achieve an over-arching overview of the process required to do this. Resulting from the author's own empirical research investigation, the Knowledge Cube offers a model of knowledge creation for the virtual web environment. A table of characteristics and skills required for an online moderator to manage design and facilitate the knowledge-focused web environment has also been presented.

Table 13.1	Valuing and exploiting your personal knowledge capital

PKC – Internal	**PKC – External**
Exploiting PKC tacitness at the individual level through:	Facilitating PKC at the external level through:
<ul><li>Listening to the heart</li><li>Listening through alertness</li><li>Knowingness, know-how</li><li>Observation</li><li>Sensing</li><li>Instinct and gut feel</li><li>Intuition</li><li>Feeling along the emotional scale</li><li>Assessing</li><li>Self-talk, and observing thoughts, and mind imprint</li><li>Reflection</li><li>Being and authenticity</li><li>Personal awareness</li></ul>	<ul><li>Interactive web environment</li><li>Creating a web infrastructure</li><li>Creating an ecology</li><li>Managing and designing for IC and social capital in virtual communities</li><li>Valuing conversation</li><li>Managing conversation</li><li>Reflecting in blogs and journals</li><li>Building networks</li><li>Valuing relationships</li><li>Valuing strength of ties within relationships</li><li>Developing trust</li><li>Being aware of culture</li></ul>

Summary

A heightened sense of awareness of the concept of 'inner and outer' personal knowledge capital may help you tenfold to deal with everyday life. It helps you steer yourself in the right direction. Personal knowledge capital, with its emphasis on inner and outer aspects of knowledge, supports a view of developing knowledge creation which includes self-development, personal awareness and a conceptual understanding of the infrastructure and ecologies required to exploit deep knowledge. In this way, it enables us to delve into our own natural inner knowledge, as well as enabling us to exploit and develop outer levels of knowledge. The inner in terms of how we tap into our own personal potential, and the outer, in terms of how we interact with the outside world. This forms part of a synthesis of mind verse body thinking in relation to knowledge creation theory within knowledge management theory. It is the hope of the author that making best use of inner techniques will become acceptable practice in the future. In a world where technology increasingly dominates, understanding this timeless wisdom becomes more important than ever. As greater inner awareness develops, it is imperative that there are obvious routes in which to communicate this valuable knowledge in the workplace. The outer web world enables us to work smarter, communicate faster, share ideas at breakneck speed and use technology for mass communication. Moreover, it is suggested that value is created by using all the tools and techniques currently available. Personal knowledge capital focuses on using smart technology to support social capital creation. Frameworks and models have been proposed throughout to help the knowledge worker use these techniques for outer knowledge capital. The blend of 'inner and outer' knowledge capital makes for a wise knowledge worker, who can use every aspect available to them, including head, heart and body to move forward in the corporate environment. In this way, knowledge workers can integrate their inner personal awareness with outer aspects of knowledge capital concept in a balanced way, to carry out their activities at work, in order to produce innovative and creative solutions to work-based issues and problems.

Glossary

Ba	Time and space nexus
Basho	Collective set of Ba
Co-ka	Cooperative and collective (group level) usage of inner knowledge
Ka	Inner knowledge awareness within the individual
KCAs	Knowledge Creation Assets
KM	Knowledge management
LOFT	Model for – listen, observe, feel, think
PKC	Personal knowledge capital
PKM	Personal knowledge management
PKMS	Personal knowledge management systems
SECI	Socialisation, externalisation, combination, internalisation

References

Abrams LC, Cross R, Lesser E and Levin DZ (2003) Nurturing interpersonal trust in knowledge — sharing networks. *Academy of Management Executives*, Vol. 17, No. 4.

Agnihotri R and Troutt MD (2009) The effective use of technology in personal knowledge management: A framework of skills, tools and user context. *Online Information Review*, Vol. 33, No. 2, pp. 329–42.

Allee V (1997) *The knowledge evolution: Expanding organisational intelligence*. New York: Butterworth-Heinemann.

Amidon DM (2003) *The innovation superhighway: Harnessing intellectual capital for sustainable collaborative advantage*. New York: Butterworth-Heinemann.

Choo and Bontis (2002) cited in Gourlay S (2006) Conceptualizing knowledge creation: A critique of Nonaka's theory. *Journal of Management Studies*, Vol. 43, No. 7 (November).

Chopra D (2004) *The book of secrets*. London: Random House.

Chopra D (2008) Seduction of the Spirit Retreat. Dublin, Ireland, July 2008.

Cope M (2000) *Know your value? Value what you know.* London: FT/Prentice-Hall.

Cope M (2003) *Personal networking: How to make your connections count.* London: FT/Prentice-Hall.

Davis cited in Amidon DM (2003) *The innovation superhighway. Harnessing intellectual capital for sustainable collaborative advantage.* London: Butterworth-Heinemann.

Doong HS and Wang HC (2008) Predicators of diverse usage behaviour towards personal knowledge management systems. *Online Information Review*, Vol. 33, No. 2, pp. 316–28.

Drucker PF (1999) *Management challenges for the twenty-first century.* Oxford: Butterworth-Heinemann.

Dvir R and Pashner E (2004) Innovative engines for knowledge cities: an innovation ecology perspective. *Journal of Knowledge Management*, Vol. 8, No. 5.

Easterby-Smith and Lyles (2003) cited in Gourlay S (2006) Conceptualizing knowledge creation: A critique of Nonaka's theory. *Journal of Management Studies*, Vol. 43, No. 7.

Edvinsson (1997) cited in McElroy MW (2003) *The new knowledge management: Complexity, learning and sustainable innovation.* New York: Butterworth-Heinemann.

Efimova L (2010) The European Knowledge Board, January. *www.knowledgeboard.com*

Fredrickson B (2011) *Positivity: Groundbreaking research to release your inner optimists and thrive.* Oxford: Oneworld.

Garcia BC (2009) Developing connectivity: A PKM path for higher education workplace learners. *Online Information Review*, Vol. 33, No. 2, pp. 276–97.

Goleman D (1996) *Working with Emotional Intelligence.* London: Bloomsbury.

Gourlay S (2006) Conceptualizing knowledge creation: A critique of Nonaka's theory. *Journal of Management Studies*, Vol. 43, No. 7 (November).

Gunawardena CN, Ortegano-Layne L, Carabajal K, Frechette C, Lindemann K and Jennings B (2006) New model, new strategies: Instructional design for wisdom communities. *Distance Education*, Vol. 27, No. 2, Issue 1, pp. 17–22.

Hardaker G and Smith DE (2002) E-learning communities, virtual markets and knowledge creation. *European Business Review*, Vol. 14, No. 5, pp. 342–50.

Hay, L (1991) *The power is within you*. London and New Delhi: Hay House Inc.

Higgison S (2004) cited in Agnihotri R and Troutt MD (2009) The effective use of technology in personal knowledge management: A framework of skills, tools and user content. *Online Information Review*, Vol. 33, No. 2, pp. 329–42.

Huysman M and Wulf V (2006) IT to support knowledge sharing in communities: Towards a social capital analysis. *Journal of Information Technology*, Vol. 21, No. 1, pp. 40–51.

Jefferson (2006) cited in Jones R (2009) Personal knowledge management through communicating. *Online Information Review*, Vol. 33, No. 2, pp. 225–36.

Jones R (2009) Personal knowledge management through communicating. *Online Information Review*, Vol. 33, No. 2, pp. 225–36.

Kok A (2007) Intellectual capital management as part of knowledge management initiatives at institutions of higher learning. *The Electronic Journal of Knowledge Management*, Vol. 5, No. 2, pp. 181–92. Available online at *www.ejikm.com*

Kolb DA (1976; 1981; 1984) *Experiential learning: Experience at the source of learning and development*. Upper Saddle River, NJ: Prentice-Hall.

Lang CJ (2004) Social context and social capital as enablers of knowledge integration. *Journal of Knowledge Management*, Vol. 8, No. 3, pp. 89–105.

Laurillard D (2007) *Rethinking university education: A framework for the effective use of learning technologies.* London and New York: RoutledgeFalmer.

Li M and Gao F (2003) Why Nonaka highlights tacit knowledge: A critical review. *Journal of Knowledge Management*, Vol. 7, No. 4, pp. 6–14.

McConnell C and Cope M (2001) *Float you: How to capitalize on your talent.* London and New York: FT/Prentice-Hall.

McDermott R (1999a) Why information technology inspired but cannot deliver knowledge management. *California Management Review*, Summer, Vol. 4, No. 4.

McDermott R (1999b) Nurturing three-dimensional communities of practice: How to get the most out of human networks. *Knowledge Management Review*, Nov.–Dec.

McDermott R and O'Dell C (2001) Overcoming cultural barriers to sharing knowledge. *Journal of Knowledge Management*, Vol. 5, No. 1, pp. 76–85.

McElroy MW (2003) *The new knowledge management: Complexity, learning and sustainable innovation.* London: Butterworth-Heinemann.

Maier R (2007) *Knowledge management systems: Information and communication technologies for knowledge management.* Heidelberg: Springer Verlag.

Maier R and Sametinger J (2004) Peer-to-peer information workspaces in Infotop. *International Journal of Software Engineering and Knowledge Engineering*, Vol. 14, No. 1, pp. 79–102.

Martin cited in Garcia Blanca C (2009) Developing connectivity: A PKM path for higher education workplace learners. *Online Information Review*, Vol. 33, No. 2, pp. 276–97.

Miller (2005) cited in Jones R (2009) Personal knowledge management through communicating. *Online Information Review*, Vol. 33, No. 2, pp. 225–36.

Mynatt ED, Adler VL, Ilto A and O'Day M (1997) Network communities: something old, something new, something borrowed. *Computer Supported Collaborative Work*, Vol. 7, No. 34, pp. 123–56.

Nahapiet J and Ghoshal S (1998) Social capital, intellectual capital and the creation of value in firms. *Academy of Management*, Vol. 23, No. 2.

Nonaka I (1991) The knowledge creation company. *Harvard Business Review*, No. 69, Nov.–Dec., pp. 96–104.

Nonaka I and Konno N (1998) The concept of 'ba' building a foundation for knowledge creation. *California Management Review*, Vol. 40, No. 3, pp. 1–15.

Nonaka I and Reinmoeller P (2000) *Dynamic business systems for knowledge creation and utilization* cited in Despres C and Chauvel D (2000) *Knowledge horizons: The present and the promise of knowledge*. Boston: Butterworth-Heinemann.

Nonaka I and Takeuchi H (1995) *The knowledge creating company: How Japanese companies create the dynamics of innovation*. Oxford and New York: Oxford University Press.

Nonaka I, Byosiere P, Borucki C and Konno N (1994) Organizational knowledge creation theory: A first comprehensive test. *International Business Review*, Vol. 3, No. 4, pp. 337–51.

Nonaka I, Reinmoeller LP and Toyama R (2001) Integrated IT systems for knowledge creation in *The Handbook of Organizational Learning and Knowledge* eds M Dierkes, A Berthoin Antal, J Child and I Nonaka. New York: Oxford University Press, pp. 827–48.

Nonaka I, Toyama R and Konno N (2000) SECI, ba and leadership: A unified model of dynamic knowledge creation. *Long Range Planning*, Vol. 33, pp. 5–34.

Paramahansa Yogananda (1946) *The autobiography of a yogi*. Los Angeles: International Publications Council of Self-Realization Fellowship.

Paramahansa Yogananda (1982) *Man's eternal quest*. Ranchi, Jharkhand: Yogoda Satsanga Society of India.

Payne (1999) cited in Jones R (2009) Personal knowledge management through communicating. *Online Information Review*, Vol. 33, No. 2, pp. 225–36.

Polanyi M (1966; 1983) *The tacit dimension*. Garden City, NY: Doubleday & Co.

Renzl R (2008) Trust in management and knowledge sharing: The mediating effects of fear and knowledge documentation. *The International Journal of Management Science*, Vol. 36, No. 2, pp. 206–20.

Roach MG (2000) *The diamond cutter: The Buddha on managing your business and your life*. New York: Doubleday.

Ruiz DM (2004) *The voice of knowledge*. San Rafael, CA: Amber-Allen Publishing.

Ryde R (2007) *Thought leadership: moving hearts and minds*. Basingstoke: Palgrave Macmillan.

Saint-Onge H (1996) Tacit knowledge: The key to strategic alignment of intellectual capital. *Strategy and Leadership*, March–April.

Sartre J-P (1976) cited in Boyle M (2005) Sartre's circular dialectic and the emphasis of abstract space: A history of space and place in Ballymun, Dublin. Paper from the Dept of Geography and Sociology, University of Strathclyde.

Sbarcea (2001) cited in Weir D and Hutchings K (2005) Cultural embeddedness and contextual constraints: Knowledge sharing in Chinese and Arab cultures. *Knowledge and Process Management*, Vol. 12, No. 2, pp. 89–98.

Schein EH (1985; 1992) *Organizational culture and leadership*. San Francisco: Jossey-Bass.

Schon DA (1983) *The reflective practitioner: How professionals think in action.* Aldershot: Ashgate Publishing.

Scott (2005) cited in Garcia Blanca C (2009) Developing connectivity: A PKM path for higher education workplace learners. *Online Education Review*, Vol. 33, No. 2, pp. 276–97.

Seligman MEP (2004) *Authentic happiness: Using the new positive psychology to realize your potential for lasting fulfilment.* London: Nicholas Brearley.

Senge PM, Scharmer CO, Jaworski J and Flowers BS (2005) *Presence: An exploration of profound change in people, organisations, and society.* London: Nicholas Brearley.

Sharma R (2003; 2008) *The monk who sold his Ferrari: A fable about fulfilling your dreams and reaching your destiny.* Delhi: JAICO Publishing House.

Sharma R (2010) *Leadership wisdom.* London and New York: Harper Element.

Skryme DJ (1999) *Knowledge networking: Creating the collaborative enterprise.* Oxford and New York: Butterworth-Heinemann.

Snowden D (2000) *The social ecology of knowledge management* cited in Despres C and Chauvel D (2000) *Knowledge horizons: The present and the promise of knowledge management.* Boston: Butterworth-Heinemann.

Snowden D (2000) Cynefin: A sense of time and place: An ecological approach to sense making and informal communities. Paper delivered to OR KMAC 2000 conference, Birmingham.

Snowden D (2005) Speaker at International Conference on Knowledge Culture and Change, Rhodes, Greece, July.

Stewart TA (1998) *Intellectual capital: The new wealth of organisations.* London: Nicholas Brearley.

Sveiby KE (1997) *The new organizational wealth: Managing and measuring knowledge-based assets*. Brisbane: Berrett-Koehler.

Truch E (2001) Managing personal knowledge: The key to tomorrow's employability. *Journal of Change Management*, Vol. 2, No. 2.

Von Krogh G, Ichijo K and Nonaka I (2000) *Enabling knowledge creation: How to unlock the mystery of tacit knowledge and release the power of innovation*. Oxford and New York: Oxford University Press.

Weir D and Hutchings K (2005) Cultural embeddedness and contextual constraints: Knowledge sharing in Chinese and Arab cultures. *Knowledge and Process Management*, Vol. 12, No. 2, pp. 89–98.

Wenger (1998) cited in Huysman M and Wulf V (2006) IT to support knowledge sharing in communities: Towards a social capital analysis. *Journal of Information Technology*, Vol. 21, No. 2, pp. 40–51.

Wenger E (2000) Communities of practice and social learning systems. *Organisation*, Vol. 7, No. 2, pp. 225–46.

Wenger E, McDermott R and Snyder WM (2002) *Cultivating communities of practice*. Boston, MA: Harvard Business School Press.

Wright (2005) cited in Jones R (2009) Personal knowledge management through communicating. *Online Information Review*, Vol. 33, No. 2, pp. 329–42.

Young J (2007) Personal knowledge management, lecture series at Northumbria University.

Young J (2009) The development of a knowledge creation framework for learning environments in higher education using web environments. Ph.D. thesis, Northumbria University.

Young J (2009) Knowledge and learning frameworks: the cyclical model of knowledge and learning and the

Knowledge Cube for higher education — a case study. *International Journal of Knowledge Culture and Change*, Vol. 9, No. 10.

Yuan YC, Gay G and Hembrooke H (2006) Focused activities and the development of social capital in a distributed learning 'community'. *The Information Society*, Vol. 22, pp. 25–39.

Index

Printed and bound by CPI Group (UK) Ltd, Croydon, CR0 4YY

08/05/2025

01864973-0004